theatre & history

Theatre &
Series Editors: Jen Harvie and Dan Rebellato

theatre &
history

Rebecca Schneider

methuen | drama

LONDON · NEW YORK · OXFORD · NEW DELHI · SYDNEY

METHUEN DRAMA
Bloomsbury Publishing Plc
50 Bedford Square, London, WC1B 3DP, UK
1385 Broadway, New York, NY 10018, USA
29 Earlsfort Terrace, Dublin 2, Ireland

BLOOMSBURY, METHUEN DRAMA and the Diana logo are trademarks
of Bloomsbury Publishing Plc

First published in Great Britain 2014 by Palgrave Macmillan
Reprinted by Methuen Drama 2022

A catalogue record for this book is available from the British Library.

A catalog record for this book is available from the Library of Congress.

Schneider, Rebecca.
    Theatre & history / Rebecca Schneider.
       pages cm.—(Theatre and)
    Includes bibliographical references and index.
    ISBN 978–0–230–24661–4
    1. Historical drama – History and criticism. 2. Literature and history.
    3. Historical reenactments. I. Title. II. Title: Theatre and history.
PN1872.S35 2014
791.6'24—dc23

                                                              2014021336

ISBN: PB: 978-0-230-24661-4

contents

series editors' preface

The theatre is everywhere, from entertainment districts to the fringes, from the rituals of government to the ceremony of the courtroom, from the spectacle of the sporting arena to the theatres of war. Across these many forms stretches a theatrical continuum through which cultures both assert and question themselves.

Theatre has been around for thousands of years, and the ways we study it have changed decisively. It's no longer enough to limit our attention to the canon of Western dramatic literature. Theatre has taken its place within a broad spectrum of performance, connecting it with the wider forces of ritual and revolt that thread through so many spheres of human culture. In turn, this has helped make connections across disciplines; over the past fifty years, theatre and performance have been deployed as key metaphors and practices with which to rethink gender, economics, war, language, the fine arts, culture and one's sense of self.

Theatre & is a long series of short books which hopes to capture the restless interdisciplinary energy of theatre and performance. Each book explores connections between theatre and some aspect of the wider world, asking how the theatre might illuminate the world and how the world might illuminate the theatre. Each book is written by a leading theatre scholar and represents the cutting edge of critical thinking in the discipline.

We have been mindful, however, that the philosophical and theoretical complexity of much contemporary academic writing can act as a barrier to a wider readership. A key aim for these books is that they should all be readable in one sitting by anyone with a curiosity about the subject. The books are challenging, pugnacious, visionary sometimes and, above all, clear. We hope you enjoy them.

Jen Harvie and Dan Rebellato

theatre & history

Since you are holding it in your hand (or using your hand to scroll across your screen), you are already aware that three words put together make the title of this little book – *Theatre & History*. In fact, the order of the first and third words may not matter very much. What is important – it seems obvious – is that the ampersand, the coordinating conjunction "and," falls in the middle. It's in the middle that things often get interesting. But it's also where things can get awkward or confusing.

Given that this book is part of a *Theatre &* series of books, the "and" may function here not only as a coordinating conjunction, but as what's called a copulative conjunction. In a copulative conjunction, one of the words is an add-on, or surplus in some way, and as in all copulation, things can get sticky, complicated, and lead to all sorts of family disputes. Which comes first, for instance – theatre *or* history? Which is on top, which on bottom, in order of interest, emphasis, importance, pleasure, and so on?

But let's not let squabbles start before we even begin!

Most of the book that follows will be about the amper-sand — the conjoining "and" that brings together, for the time we spend together in this book, *theatre* and *history*. It is not a book of theatre history, or even about theatre history,[1] but a book balancing in the sometimes awkward overlap-ping spaces between the practices, between the disciplines, between the ideas and ends of theatre and history. When we fall fully into the topic, as we will, we may at times feel far removed from the most grounded question: Why?

Why study theatre and history?

It seems as if we ought to proceed with care. Because, in fact, the topic is one of importance. This is not a small book on a conjunction rarely studied by students — say, theatre and seagulls, or Vulcans and history. Almost every Theatre Department in every major university in Europe and the United States offers a course or courses on thea-tre history, often as a requirement for those who gradu-ate with the focus of their degree in Theatre Arts. Even if History Departments do not regularly offer theatre history as a requirement, we might add ruefully, the topic is never-theless one with gravitas, with its own history and its own ongoing theatre of operations.

Still, for some students, particularly those who want to go onto the stage as actors, studying theatre history can feel like sitting on your hands.

For others, such as those who study history, getting on your feet to "act" may seem antithetical to proper archival pursuits or engagement with fact.

The two don't often know why they might want to be in conversation.

For most practitioners, the theatre is "live," and by definition "now." History appears at first glance to be neither. Doesn't a theatre artist struggle to lift calcified worlds *off* of the page or *out* of the past? Being in the moment, finding the "beat," chasing intuition, riding "emotion memory," or even just "finding your light" – how can that possibly be related to spelunking for "facts" in dark and dusty archives where historians work like Shakespeare's burrowing old moles (Harries 2000: 81)?

Conversely, for historians, studying a medium in its liveness, its "nowness," may seem against the grain of the project of history – a project that, by most accounts, seeks to analyze the "then" in some distinction to the "now." Even if a history brings us "up to the minute," few historians would claim it's the minute shared by the reader in a "co-presence" akin to theatre (Zhao 2004; Fischer-Lichte 2008). "What happened" does not recur.[2] What's in the past stays in the past. Can the dead appear live? The live dead? Then and now are not usually given to be simultaneous, except in decidedly problematic embodied practices – like reenactment and theatre.

To historians, actors may seem like the manipulators of shadows in Plato's proverbial cave, their surface projections at a definite remove from anything resembling ideal or real historical evidence concerning whatever is presented. It may seem against best practice to look to the theatre – the domain of artifice – for what happened in a past "reality."

Theatre can only "evidence" theatre — a *mise en abyme* that doesn't ever hit the ground of the real. Isn't theatre, and theatricality, always essentially faux? Thinking with and through the theatrical can raise conundrums almost beyond measure whenever "facts" are at stake. If one can say a production of *The Seagull* by Anton Chekhov "happened" in 1898 at the Moscow Art Theatre, what relation would the real falseness of the theatre have, or have had, to the real reality of the street, the city, the country, the world of actual events? Beyond the recognition that people, "then," made theatre "then" (and that that "then" was "now" only "then"), why study it further? The now and the then, the pretend and the real, are awkward bedfellows at best, and aren't the progeny of their copulation complicated hybrids? Impossibilities? Illegitimacies? Errors?

So, I've decided to start this small book with brief sections on the words themselves — "And," "History," "Theatre" — followed by sections on why the topic is important. Dropping the "and" would leave us with "Theatre History." It is useful, I think, to ask quite simply: Why study it? And important, as well, to ask that question both for students of theatre and for students of history, though in fact it is not only students who sometimes wonder at this conjunction, but teachers and professional practitioners as well as audiences of both disciplines. Sometimes it's the most obvious things that require the greatest patience to think through. So, after we've looked at how the dictionary might orient our use of the words, we'll drop the "and" for a moment to turn to the topic: Why study theatre history?

This important question is taken up in two sections, each with subsections. The first, "History and the theatre artist," is addressed to theatre artists. The second, "Theatre and the historian," is addressed to historians. But my hope, of course, is that the deleted ampersand continues its copulative activities under wraps, so to speak, and that the borders will begin to blur as we see some of the same anxieties, problems, hopes, desires, and aims occurring from different directions in both perspectives. When we return to the ampersand, we will already be well aware of the tangled terrain between the terms, and well into the heat of our ... activities.

For the moment, then, before the important question of "Why?," let's get down to the matter of what the words assembled for study actually mean. A warning in advance: looking closely at the dictionary does not, in fact, simplify our pursuit. Quite the contrary!

"And"

"And," the *Oxford English Dictionary* tells us, is "simply connective."[3] With this word, one thing – theatre – is "simply" given to exist in relation to another thing – history. But what relation? And how simple?

In truth, a connecting preposition might have been simpler than "and." Think of the straightforwardness of various prepositions that might have been used to suggest relation. For example, "Theatre *in* History." That phrase would signal the various practices of theatre that have happened in the past and would not indicate an open relation. Theatre would be placed *inside* the ongoing stream of events in time, and such a book could relate facts about which theatres did what, when, where, why, and how in the flow of historical time. Or, if we went a step further in thinking about theatre in history, the preposition "in" might signify the theatrical properties of historiography itself — the theatrical or fictive in historical writing. Or we could flip the first and third words around the "in" for a very different meaning, a different outside and inside: "History in Theatre." That phrase might indicate, straightforwardly, historical facts as they are transmitted on stage — what history looks like, sounds like, feels like replayed in a theatre.

The phrase "Theatre *as* History" would be another example. It would seem to suggest that theatre can be approached as a mode of telling or making or displaying the past, just as the phrase "History as Theatre" might suggest the argument that any written narrative about the past is always a substitution or surrogate — posing for the thing itself — and in that way theatrical. Think about "History *of* Theatre." Or "Theatre of History." Both phrases appear to be far more straightforward in terms of the relation that is set up between the words. But "simply" connective, "Theatre *and* History" tells us nothing about the connection. Whether in comparison or in distinction, *just what the relation is* goes unsaid.

Our task, then, is to say what we might say about theatre *and* history and the practices they signify — in relation and in distinction. What we will find is rarely if ever a simple relation, and neither is any distinction entirely easy to draw. There are quite a few complexities held tenuously in the "simple" ampersand and those complexities are always interesting – if, at times, infuriatingly paradoxical.

We will shortly delve into all manner of complications, but as a start, and at the level of the ampersand, maybe the connection between theatre and history can be simple if we keep in mind one thing – time. Because theatre, like history, is an art of time. Even, we could say, *the* art of time. Time is the stuffing of the stage – it's what actors, directors, and designers manipulate together. In this they are much like historians who wrestle or coax or otherwise prompt sentences into place, lifting one time into another time, to say something about yesterday today. In both endeavors, time is decidedly porous, pockmarked with other times. Whenever citation or repetition is in play – as it inevitably is with gestures, stances, and words – something akin to theatre and something akin to history takes place. For to use a word is to use it again. To make a gesture or express a feeling almost immediately couples with other gestures, other feelings, from other times and places. Language itself, whether composed of ink, light, sound, or bodily gesture, teems with other times, and words other than nonsense words (and even a lot of nonsense words) set up historical relations. Words have been used before, heard before – that's how we come to understand them and "do things" with them (Austin 1975). Beforeness is a given, and beforeness (as well as afterness) is the explicit substance of rehearsal, as much as it is of archives. Theatre makes itself in the "again and again and again" that is not only rehearsal but the run of a show and the trajectory of a tradition, mode, or style of performance. History, too, goes back (and back and back) over tracks traveled before. If beforeness is relatively implicit in everyday life (Connerton 1989; Schechner 2013: 34), it is the explicit glue in the works of theatre's stages and history's pages (Roach 1993: 16–17).

Nevertheless, the couple can sometimes have trouble conversing. An acting student explained to me once that studying theatre history is a "time suck." And for an historian to take an acting class? It may be a fanciful pastime (versus past time) at best, but hardly a required tool in an historian's box of methods to access the past. And yet, studying across this divide should be vital to both endeavors. Why?

We will need to look at the "why" from a theatre student's perspective as well as the perspective of a history student. We will do that. First, though, let's stay with the idea that the relation is "simple" before we turn again to the dictionary to excavate precision. As a simple start, what do we know at a commonsense level about what these words signify? Is it possible to say a few simple things about what will soon become an impossible paradox of a project? What can we say very reductively? For example, can we say that both theatre and history are practices? That is simple enough.

You can practice theatre. You can practice history. Both are practices.

But what kind of practices are they?

What can we say of theatre as a practice? We can say, for the moment, that one can practice theatre as an actor, or dancer, or director, or designer, or spectator, or script reader, or playwright, or box office manager, or stage manager (the list goes on and on). One can practice theatre arts by renting or buying or building or finding a stage or an arena or even a street corner or URL for performance and then by performing there – rehearsing or performing a play script, or practicing improvisation, or, through one of innumerable methods, acting or directing or dancing or singing or writing or designing plays or skits or choreographies or stances or sounds or performance acts for or in that space.

What can we say of history as a practice – again, at an impossibly reductive level? We can say that one can practice history by studying the past and writing a narrative about it, or creating an oral narrative about the past based on one's own experience or on the testimonies of others, or remembering and in some way relating something about the past based on factual evidence, or researching the past in an archive or at an archaeological dig or by talking to people who experienced something in the past ... This list, too, goes on and on. One can practice history as an archivist to preserve the past, or as an archaeologist to reveal artifacts from the past and then analyze them in a narrative, or as a researcher to analyze and tell about the past, or as a curator to display the past. Uncovering, preserving, analyzing, writing about, telling about, displaying materials considered to be of the past are the domain of the historian.

So far, they are both practices. But there is overlap here. You might say of theatre, as we said of history, that you can practice theatre by analyzing, revealing, writing, telling, or displaying and that, by virtue of training and rehearsal and the practice of citation, theatre, too, necessarily processes and preserves the past. In any run of a show, the effort is usually to play the performance or perform the play as determined in rehearsal, and sometimes to present the play with "fidelity" to the author's intention, or to "original" productions, or simply according to an event score or plan, and other such temporally removed indicators of lineage or tradition or (to borrow a word from Yoko Ono) instruction. Thus, there is often a fundamental "replay" aspect to theatre and performance; whether fidelitous or infidelitous to the past, it is often the past that is put into play. In fact, this is true of any time-based art that follows a script, a score, a tradition, a style of playing, or an instruction for doing. Often a theatre artist uses or manipulates embodied traditions of theatre art (preserved through live practice and in-bodied knowledge passed down through generations) to impart stories on the stage, and more often than not those stories or plays come from a time before the present moment of production.

But let's not get too far ahead of ourselves. The word "live" has already slipped into this book several times and it will have a world of impact. For there is nothing "simple" about the appellation "live" — especially in the context of the question of what constitutes history and what constitutes theatre. Is theatre always only live? Is history … not live? If so, is it "dead"? Or if the antonym to "live" is "recorded," is history never accessed *off* the record? Or is live theatre never itself a means of recording? Can there be no body-to-body transmission that has historical verity? Can live modes of remembering, such as orature,[4] never be considered history? We're falling into a world of troubles very quickly here. Let's return to the simpler line of questioning, at least for a little while longer.

What else can we say by way of simple comparison?

Surely we can say with confidence that there are professions assigned to both practices of theatre and practices of history—if history for the moment means the art or practice of writing or telling about the past in the form of a book or narrative or record (more on this anon), and theatre means the art or practice of mounting, writing, or telling stories or acts in a space that can be called a stage or performance space (more on this anon). One can make a living as a theatre artist or theatre scholar. One can make a living as an historian. One can even make a living as a theatre historian! But: Can one make a living as the inverse of a theatre historian? And what would that be? A history theatrician? A history theatrical (for one definition of "theatrical" in the *OED* is "a professional actor")? A history performer? Or a *theatrical* historian? A performing historian? A history theatre artist? If so, what is history theatre or history performance? Again, we may be getting ahead of ourselves.

In a moment we will need to become more precise about our word use, clearly. The word "historical" and the word "theatrical," as well as the odd word "theatrician," not to mention again the word "live," have all snuck into our comparison without adequate definition. But for now, the answer to the question "Can one make a living as a history theatre artist?" might be, simply, yes. One can make a living as a history theatre artist, as awkward as the phrase may be. Think of a professional reenactor — there are quite a few Abraham Lincoln presenters out there, for example, some of whom make at least a partial living out of what for others is a "hobby."[5] Think of "performers" (if that is the right word) who engage in orature, especially those from cultures that maintain oral transmission as a form of history. Or, you might add, one can make a living as a theatre or dance practitioner who specializes in reconstruction, or as someone who practices educational performance in the heritage industry, such as first-person reenactors at history theme parks or history museums and the like. But in truth, it is at this point that the simplicity of the relation, at least in terms of professions, potentially breaks down and debate begins to rage. Is a professional playing or presenting an historical figure necessarily an historian at work? If someone researching then writing the history of theatre, or even the history of the way Lincoln himself "performed" his duties — if that person is clearly and inarguably an historian at work, what about someone researching then *playing* an historical character performing his duties? *Playing*? Can history be in play — and especially in theatrical play?[6]

If an historian acting in a play or taking part in a theatrical reenactment would still be practicing the art of theatre, the inverse does not necessarily follow: a reenactor or theatre actor might be on shaky ground if she claimed to be practicing the art of history. Is the art of history necessarily delimited to historio*graphy* – that is, "graphic," as the *OED* tells us, "drawn with a pencil or pen"? Is the art of history necessarily the art of *writing* history?

Now may be a good moment to return more fully to the dictionary. We'll start with the word "history" and move on from there to the word "theatre."

"History"

As defined by the *Oxford English Dictionary*, history is:

> **I.1.a.** A written narrative constituting a contin-
> uous chronological record of important or public
> events (esp. in a particular place) or of a particu-
> lar trend, institution, or person's life. Common
> in the titles of books.

Clearly, the first stab at a definition turns up writing as *the* modus operandi for history. The word "record" is promi-nent as well. History relies upon records, verifiable traces of the past that can be analyzed by an historian, and these records are sometimes understood in distinction to "mem-ory," which is not reliant on material records.[7] In fact, the distinction between history and prehistory largely con-cerns the existence of remains identifiable as "truthful" or verifiable "records."[8] But what is a truthful record? Can the living body be a recording machine, or a means of recording at all transmissible over time? And, even more thorny an issue, what are "historical facts" that could be said to correspond only to disembodied records?[9]

The definition at I.2.a. is only slightly different, and the word "record" is prominent again:

> **I.2.a.** The branch of knowledge that deals with past events; the formal record or study of past events, esp. human affairs. Also: this as a subject of study.

Interestingly, under I.3. we come upon a definition that is now outmoded, or "rare," and this definition includes the oral recitation, even the singing, of texts:

> **I.3.** *Christian Church.* Originally: a reading or set of liturgical readings, usually taken from the Old Testament. Later (*hist.*): the responsory or set of responsories corresponding to this; (hence) any of these sets of readings together with their responsories. Now *rare*.

A responsory is a liturgical chant traditionally consisting of a series of calls and responses said or sung by a cantor and choir alternately. So by this definition, though we are told it is *rare*, oral transmission in liturgical ritual is history, and might be related by the copulative conjunction to theatre (certainly, ritual and theatre are closely conjoined twins throughout the history of Christianity, as many theatre history textbooks explicitly relate). And in fact, the list of definitions continues in the *OED* to include "an event or story related pictorially" as well as the "facts relating to animals, plants, or other natural objects," as in "natural history."

So far, thanks to the dictionary, we are gathering written narratives, records, pictures, readings, facts, and natural objects into our definition basket. But at II.7. we are handed a basket the size of the past itself. For "history" also means:

> **II.7.a.** The whole series of past events connected with a particular person, country, institution, or thing.
> **II.7.b.** The aggregate of past events; the course of human affairs.

Here the *OED* reminds us that "history" also refers to the events themselves – the past itself – not just what is written about it, not just how it remains for the archive. Thus the same word – "history" – means two arguably different things. Is what happened the same as the record of or narrative about what happened? Is "history" (I.1.a.) the same as "history" (II.7.a.)? Is the tale told about it the same as the "it" itself? The word for both is the same, but as we all know about words – they are not the things themselves (except, perhaps, for the word "word"). Still, the relationship between word and thing is treacherously thorny and difficult to untangle *if* we are attempting to communicate with each other about the past, the present, the future – or anything else.

"A rose by any other name would smell as sweet." So said Shakespeare through Juliet in *Romeo and Juliet*. But he also said, through Feste the Clown in a short repartee with Viola in *Twelfth Night*:

> **Clown:** A sentence is but a cheveril glove to a good wit: how quickly the wrong side may be turned outward!
>
> **Viola:** Nay, that's certain: they that dally nicely with words may quickly call them wanton.
>
> **Clown:** I would therefore my sister had no name, sir.
>
> **Viola:** Why, man?
>
> **Clown:** Why, sir, her name's a word; and to dally with that word might make my sister wanton. But indeed, words are very rascals since bonds disgraced them.
>
> (III.i.12–24)

For Juliet, the name of a rose doesn't matter to the properties of a rose itself. But in the Clown's world, the way the name is used can make a rose smell sweeter, or make a sister … a tart. And of course, on Shakespeare's stage (if we know anything about theatre history), Viola would have been a boy actor cross-dressed to play a female character who cross-dresses to act as a boy. Juliet, too, is a female character – but a male actor by another name. And if we know about the history of language use, we know that in Renaissance England "glove" could be a euphemism for genitals – turned one way (inward) or the other way (outward) (Greenblatt 1989: 81, 90; Stallybrass and Jones 2001). In any case, concerning the double meaning of the word "history," perhaps the two perspectives are flipsides of the same glove. History is written about history that happened, but the writing becomes, itself, history – the writing *happens* – brings history into being in and through enunciation. What can be told about what happened, and what cannot be told, exist relative to the ways we partition the senses and legitimate only the details we have learned to consider significant. Anything we give to the archive will be recomposed in a political system that Michel Foucault called "the system of its enunciability" – what will have been already said and what will be possible to say (1972: 129). Enunciation, as an utterance or speech act, happens live, of course, and is regarded from the point of view of its intelligibility to an audience, not only its fidelity to the past. Rascals, surely! We might indeed call words "actors"!

What of words like "historicity" and "historical"? Historicity, we are told, is "the fact, or quality, or character of being situated in history; esp. historical accuracy or authenticity." Under "historical" we find 1.a.: "belonging to, constituting, or of the historical nature of history; in accordance with history" and 1.b.: "belonging to or of the nature of history as opposed to fiction or legend." Here a sense of history as true, accurate, and authentic begins to congeal, and this, perhaps, is in distinction not only to myth or fiction or legend but, significantly, to anything that might be termed "theatrical." That theatre itself has a history – the story of the many, many things, persons, and events that have happened or appeared on world stages throughout time – would require reconstituting the "truth" about what happened on stage, which would be, in essence, the truth of the false, the authentic of the inauthentic, the fact of fiction. But we have yet to look closely at the definition of "theatre" to follow this through.

"Theatre"

What about the definition of "theatre"? Etymologically, the word derives from the Greek θέᾱτρον, transliterated to the Roman alphabet as *theatron*, which means "a place for viewing, especially a theatre." Under the first entry in the *Oxford English Dictionary*, we find:

> **1.a.** *Ancient Greek Hist.* and *Roman Hist.* A place constructed in the open air, for viewing dramatic plays or other spectacles.

In pride of place at 1.a. we receive the practices in ancient Greece and Rome as definitive of theatre, which may be extremely misleading when we look to global formations, not all of which privileged the written script or considered vision/spectacle to be the primary bodily sensation of the form.[10] And such a privilege of "beginning" forgets other birthing sites – Egypt, where the possibility that "dramatic" performance nested in ritual predated the emergence of theatre in Greece has been hotly debated by scholars (Leprohon 2007); India, where Sanskrit drama's emergence from such forms as Vedic hymns led scholars to debate a coterminous emergence of Greek and Indian theatre (Richmond 1990; Gupt 1994); even Paleolithic or Neolithic sites such as caves or megalithic tombs, where some argue for the "emergence of theatricality" over 20,000 years before "civilization" produced scripts, or argue that the "enigmatic signs" on Paleolithic cave walls, or Neolithic rock formations themselves, might be read as scripts of sorts (Montelle 2009; Jones 2012).

But whether or not we root the practice of theatre, like the word *theatron*, in ancient Greece or find the tangle of ritual and performance to be "theatrical" in prehistory, the dictionary soon diverges from origins as definitive. The *OED* list of definitions that follow 1.a. (I have lifted out ten of them) makes it clear that "theatre" as a word is as rascally and wanton as they come. For "theatre" can mean the following:

> **1.†d.** A circular basin of water. *Obs.*
>
> **2.a.** In modern use, An edifice specially adapted to dramatic representations; a playhouse.
>
> **2.b.** *N. Amer.* and *N.Z.* A picture theatre, cinema.
>
> **3.b.** A theatreful of spectators; the audience, or "house", at a theatre.
>
> **3.c.** [...] dramatic art as a craft, the theatrical profession.
>
> **4.** A temporary platform, dais, or other raised stage, for any public ceremony.
>
> **5.b.** A room in a hospital specially designed for surgical operations [...]

6.b. A place where some action proceeds; the scene of action.

6.c. A particular region or one of the separate regions of the world in which a war is being fought.

†**7.** A book giving a "view" or "conspectus" of some subject; a text-book, manual, treatise. *Obs.*

Of the above selection, 6.b. is the most inclusive — anywhere an "action proceeds" can be called a theatre. And thus, all the world's a stage. This might remind us of the double term "history," where both the story told about the past and the past itself are hailed by the same word. If dramatic action on stage and the site of action itself in the "real world" are flipsides of the same word, then "theatre" can trouble a desire to definitively separate "theatricality" from "reality" — an issue we will return to in the final section, "On knives and blood." In any case, for now we can note that we are still quite comfortable referring to a "theatre of war" or a "surgical theatre" (though we rarely, anymore, think of our textbook about theatre as theatre itself).

Even harder to define is the term "theatricality," and much has been written chasing after a solid definition of that famously slippery word — a word that, to quote theatre historian Erika Fischer-Lichte, can quickly lose all semblance of meaning and become "void."[11] The tautology at play in the *Oxford English Dictionary* gives us a sense of this void. Under 1.a. for "theatricality," the *OED* gives us: "The quality or character of being theatrical; theatricalness." If we then go to "theatricalness" we find: "The quality or condition of being theatrical." Then, looking up "theatrical" we find 1.a.: "Pertaining to or connected with the theatre or 'stage', or with scenic representations." The tautology seems endless, but 2. under "theatrical" may be more helpful:

> **2.** That "plays a part"; †representing or exhibiting in the manner of an actor (*obs.*); that simulates, or is simulated; artificial, affected, assumed.

Indeed, here a less tautological definition begins to take shape. The "theatrical" is that which simulates, or stands in for a thing itself. And at this point, the "theatrical" becomes quickly aligned with falsity – "artificial, affected, assumed." "Affected" is an interesting word that can refer to *feelings* as well as to false posturing, and there will be more to say about affect anon.[12] For now, we can surmise that theatricality is in some senses the opposite of historicity, where "authenticity" and "accuracy" are keystones of the concept, despite the fact that both "theatre" and "history," as words, bear traces in their definition of being both the representation of the thing and the thing itself.

History and the theatre artist

The young actor who used the phrase "time suck" had been told by a venerated acting teacher that "theatre history" is an oxymoron.

An oxymoron is a figure of speech in which two apparently contradictory words appear together — a deafening silence, an open secret, theatre history, and the living dead. "You cannot think *and* do," the same teacher had told this young actor. She reserved "doing" for the theatre and "thinking" for … she never said. In any case, the student took her proclamation to heart. He did not want to think about theatre *or* history. He mistook his acting teacher to mean avoid all intellectual pursuit in relationship to the arts — which put him in jeopardy in quite a few of his classes and unwittingly debased his own form. He wanted to "do." How could "history" be "doing"?

So, as a start, let's assume you are a student eager to go on the stage for your profession — eager to be a theatre professional in any of the myriad ways one might do so. We'll return to the mandate "Get out of your head!" or "Don't think — do!" in a moment. For now, what does it matter what the first actor — let's call him Thespis — did or did not do in ancient Greece? Or the second or third actor? Or the nth actor? Never mind what a Paleolithic human may have performed in the magnificently illustrated caves of the ice age. What does it matter how precolonial Yoruban ritual practices might inform and inflect the contemporary plays of Wole Soyinka or Gertrude Stein or Ntozake Shange or Suzan-Lori Parks in deep ways? Gertrude Stein? Stein listened to jazz in Paris and was deeply influenced by it in her playwriting, so might some inkling about jazz, its base traditions, historical relations to Africa, and the cross-continental, cross-hemispheric journeys of Africans in diaspora enliven an understanding and practice of contemporary theatre influenced by Stein, who was influenced by jazz, wherever contemporary theatre may be mounted on a stage?

The question is simple, really. Can listening to cross-temporal and cross-geographical resonances help when mounting the plays of yesterday and the plays of today, or help when learning to act in the wide spectrum of methods that make up world theatre traditions? Understanding that precolonial African practices are as vital as ancient and medieval and early modern European practices to contemporary English-language theatre – what does it matter? What do the tracks of noh drama matter in the practice of Japanese butoh today or in the early twentieth-century plays of William Butler Yeats? The *tracks* are not the moving train! Neither are they the destination. So, thinking about how Shakespeare was performed in the nineteenth century, let alone in the sixteenth century – what does any of this matter, when you want to be on the stage *tomorrow*?

A simple answer – at least the easiest answer – is that it doesn't matter.

It is entirely OK to go into the profession without an ounce of historical background, foreground, or side-ground. And many do. But if you choose that route, with your back pockets basically empty, how employable will you be for the long run of a career? Even the most recent play was likely written before the moment you audition for it, and even if the play was written yesterday, and even if you are working with a living playwright to create a play on your feet, the chances are that references to times, places, and styles will be made beyond the frame of your own life. That's what theatre does — it cites, and replays, other places and other times. Even dramas set in the future situate the future relative to the past. It's hard to get away from that fact unless you are auditioning for Reality TV, and even then there is already a performance history to the genre that informs the choices that are made (Enders 1999: 24).

Let's get even more simplistic. If you are an actor, in the daily mechanics of the profession you might be asked to prepare an audition, and let's say the play that is casting is Heiner Müller's *Hamletmachine*.

On second thought, let's stay with something that seems more straightforward. How about *The Seagull* again? Most students in the US and the UK are trained in acting styles of "naturalism" descended from the actor, director, and theatre theorist Constantin Stanislavsky, and Chekhov's *The Seagull* was first directed by Stanislavsky at the Moscow Art Theatre. So let's explore there.

Would it help to know something about Chekhov's play in advance of the audition? Obviously, it might. At least to know the part. Let's say you want to play Nina.

Well and good. Would it help to know something, in advance, about the character? But how much, aside from what "ingénue" means, should you know? Would it help to know that the family Nina is visiting (she is a visitor throughout the play) is part of the landed gentry at a moment when Russia ... yada yada blah blah blah? It might help. But in that case, why would you have to know about the history of *theatre*? Wouldn't you only have to know about the history of

Russia, or even just the most cursory bit about class relations in a rapidly industrializing nineteenth-century Europe? So, why know about the history of *theatre*?

Let's say that you arrive at your audition for *The Seagull* knowing nothing about the play or the playwright or the setting or the history of Russia or the history of Europe or the legacy of the Moscow Art Theatre (despite the fact that you're trained in naturalist acting). You've heard, perhaps, that Nina's parents are "afraid I'll want to be an actress" — and so are your own! So, there's a connection already! You've also heard that the director wants to set the play in today's New York, and if you live in New York today, you are set! Right? Let's even say the director wants to set it on Vulcan, and since no one lives on Vulcan (and Vulcan doesn't exist), no worries! But what happens when, as you read the dialog or monolog handed to you, the director stops you and asks for a bit more "naturalism" to the scene? — More natural, please!

On the one hand you might think the director means making your acting appear more true to you, as you live your life day to day. And maybe so. You've gained some technique for how to do this from your acting classes. But would it help to understand something about the theatre movement of naturalism? The aims of naturalism when Chekhov was writing? Or what naturalism came to mean in the long twentieth century? (If you are really a know-it-all, you might add that Chekhov didn't want this play to be experienced as a naturalist play, but, in truth, knowing that might not help — everyone would think you were *too* Vulcan!) In any case, the "natural" is almost always a can of worms when thought about historically. Because, in fact, the director's idea of naturalism might not be your own. Though the range of techniques and lines of lineage for training in naturalist acting are far too long a dramatic and hotly debated tale to tell here (see Davis 2001), simply knowing something about the variant and shifting grounds to naturalism (knowing something about theatre history) might help you find common and stable ground with your director.

Remember that in our story, you are auditioning for Nina. Let's say you get the part. Congratulations! What happens when the director asks for some "Symbolist" style to your intonation when Treplev directs Nina to perform in his play within the play? What will that mean to you? Chekhov's play, like many plays, calls for various theatrical styles within it, sometimes simultaneously. Being even slightly versed in the varied and sometimes tumultuous theatre histories of the nineteenth and twentieth centuries might give you some common ground when the director starts to talk to you about her vision for the twenty-first-century production you will mount together. There will be over 100 years between the script you engage and the audience you meet. And believe me, a director will talk to you about this. The director might say she is interested in peppering the play with some Brechtian or Boalian elements; certainly melodrama and Shakespearean elements are called for in the play. Or perhaps the director is looking for the flavor of Greek tragedy or Roman comedy (Chekhov's play is a "tragi-comedy") or *commedia dell'arte* and might ask you to try this or that gestural spice from an historical period or geographical tradition in the playing of a scene. When a director says "Let's get medieval on it!" she might not be quoting, or might not only be quoting, *Pulp Fiction*. How ready will you be? And I really only mean ready to negotiate the languages, not to already know everything – because a common language will be something you have to discover anew every time with every team in the theatre. So, the question really is, how flexible can you be? Theatre history can help you be, and remain, flexible.

Studying theatre beyond the theatre you are standing in at the moment expands your palette immensely in the profession when it comes time to build an ensemble. Ultimately, a grasp on the history of theatre will make you not only a good conversationalist at cocktail parties (no minor skill in the profession!), but a far more versatile performer. It is obvious, but frequently forgotten, that there are quite a few languages of the stage that predate your entry onto the scene. And though some schools prepare students in only one stage language, and many teachers or theatre programs proselytize their own method, anyone who surfs the web or watches television or goes to a film or performance installation in a gallery or museum or attends the theatre at more than one venue in more than one city and, thus, regularly sees employed actors in all manner of performances will readily acknowledge the range and flexibility required for a life in the profession. Knowing something about how to use history in the design and implementation of a production will expand your readiness immeasurably — and as Shakespeare has Hamlet say in Act V, scene ii: "readiness is all."

These examples might seem silly or over the top — and in truth, they are — and everyone knows Hamlet dies in the end, so perhaps readiness is overrated? But think of any play you know, consider the infinite choices of production, and follow the logic. "Table work" in the theatre actually involves thinking actors — the best actors at any rate have the sharpest, quickest minds and can think — *and do think* — at the table and on their feet. Unlike what the venerated acting teacher said, the best actors are nimble, even more nimble than most, with fluid passage between brain and heart, body and mind (why do we even imagine the two as separate?). And in any case, if you've studied theatre history well in advance, you can spin on a dime. Remember, you got an A-plus in theatre history! You killed it!

If you are heading into the profession as a director, the payback is enormous. What traditions precede you? There is a vast range of materials already at hand on directing techniques. What kinds of lateral and deep references can you make? How ready are you to discuss your ideas with backers or artistic directors? Students are often completely surprised at the range of humor as well as violence in medieval theatre, for example, and when they read or reread Antonin Artaud (1994) in the context of thinking about history — the medieval Black Death he resituates between the modern World Wars, strangely mixed with colonial fantasies about Balinese performance — a mind as well as a gut can buckle and swerve. Creativity actually grows better in the cracks of what you know than it does on rock solid ground – but you have to know something to have cracks in what you know. The actions and choices of artists that precede you are part of your own legacy, and those past actions and endeavors rebuckle and bend in your hands – if you know what you are doing. Without any past there is precious little juice for the future, and as the philosopher Jacques Derrida (1998) once wrote, archives lie in wait for the future, are *of* the future, even more than the past. In addition, if Stanislavsky (1989), Sigmund Freud (1990), and Michel Foucault (1977) would all agree that your own body is an archive, then embodied art necessarily puts history into collective (re)practice. Similarly, according to Dominick LaCapra (2001), being an historian is already either acting out or working (acting) through. Being an historian is always, like being an actor, in some capacity replaying.

As a director, you will ultimately hope for actors conversant with archival practices – remembering that the broad scope of what archive can mean, at least in some schools of thought, includes the body (more on this contested topic anon). It was Stanislavsky, after all, who compared an actor to a miner or an archaeologist, insofar as the actor must "dig deep" into his or her "inner resources" and employ "detailed and intricate research" for the "tiny bead" of emotion that lies hidden in the "divisions and subdivisions" of what he called an "archive" of memory (1989: 289, 188). Stanislavsky thought that this archive, and his methods of excavation, could spark a cross-temporal intrapersonal connection that brings "life" to a scene. Thus, as a director you might look for actors who come to the stage with the skills of an archivist in their toolkit. Readiness is not, after all, the same as a blank slate — at least not if there is no chalk to go with it. Even if you want to be totally shiny and new on the surface, does it help to know something of the past, and the archives (both flesh-based and object- or text-based) that might be said to house it, in order to ignore it? Knowing what you consciously chose to ignore can give you confidence, and more than enough reasons to press in a different direction. Such knowledge can only deepen your work.

The antitheatrical prejudice

Theatre students are well aware of legacies of antitheatricality that can cause their parents, like Nina's, to fear their chosen profession. Many have heard the comment: "Don't study theatre, you'll never get work." Or, "Do you really want to be a waiter?" Or, "Choose a serious profession!" Some students may have heard: "Why not major in history, dear?"

Why are parents so worried? Shakespeare's investment in the cliché *theatrum mundi* — as in "All the world's a stage / And all the men and women merely players" — may have, among other things, allowed performers to get away with searing critiques of the status quo because, after all, they are "only acting" (Greenblatt 1989: 8; Garber 2008: 292) — but many parents don't want their kids to be "merely" anything. Despite the fact that the same parents who caution their offspring against a career in performance might regularly sit those offspring in front of the TV, or take them to the theatre to "get culture," or gather as a family to watch the History Channel – that is, despite the fact that there they might daily encounter the tracks of hundreds of employed actors (more employed actors, arguably, than employed historians) – the caution against performance as a profession is still alive and well.

The standard cover-up that "you'll never find work" may actually be hiding other, older prejudices against the art form. We know the deep anxiety Plato reserved for poets and performers, and though it would be a mistake to consider Plato's writing completely antitheatrical (Halliwell 2002: 59; Puchner 2010), a strain of anxiety about mimesis runs at the core of Western "civilization." Early modern antitheatrical pamphleteers claimed that the theatre turns men into women (Levine 1994) – horrors! And eighteenth-century antitheatrical novelists feared that the theatre "turns women into actresses – those in the fashionable boxes as well as those on the stage" (Michals 2010: 191).

In fact, the historical link between theatre and debauchery, theatre and prostitution, theatre and homosexuality, theatre and impurity still holds traction. Underneath the claim that you wouldn't get work, your parents might actually fear that you *would* get work, but that the work you get might make you less than honorable or less than stable, a fear still tinged with misogyny and homophobia. The Latin *histrio* for "actor" and Greek *hustero* for "womb" are near homonyms that might be mistaken for each other. The Latin *hystericus* ("hysterical") derives from the Greek *husterikos* ("suffering in the womb, hysterical"), and the Greek word for "actor" is, after all, *hypocrites*. The strange threat of "suffering wombs" and passions out of control seems always in the wings of a long and misogynist tradition that haunts theatre art in the West as not only incapable of the purities and truths of the more elevated, more masculine and dispassionate arts and letters, but actually corrupting of those truths.

Fischer-Lichte begins her *History of European Drama and Theatre* with Jean-Jacques Rousseau's 1758 *Letter to Monsieur D'Alembert*, in which Rousseau cautions, in no uncertain terms, that theatre is gender and sexuality trouble. Moreover, it's just false:

> What is the actor's talent? The art of deception, to take on another character instead of his own, to appear other than he is, to be passionate in cold blood, to speak other than how he really thinks and to do it as naturally as if he really thinks in that way and finally to forget his own situation so much that he transforms himself into another. [...] What then is this spirit which the actor draws into himself? A mixture of baseness, falseness [...] which enables him to play all kinds of roles except the most noble which is what he abandons, the role of human being. (Cited in Fischer-Lichte 2002: 1)

Even though she argues that Rousseau's rabid form of antitheatricality is now "long obsolete," Fischer-Lichte starts with Rousseau before turning to ancient Greece. Why? Remembrance of the antitheatrical bias continues to set theatre's historical stage, even if only to allow scholars to argue, as Fischer-Lichte does, for that bias's supposed obsolescence. To know something about the history of European theatre is inevitably to know something about the history of antitheatricality. And the history of antitheatricality may be why some theatre practitioners dig in their heels and appear, as if in defensive reaction, anti-intellectual – not even recognizing, at times, their own tradition's still quite lively antitheatrical bias.

The anti-intellectual prejudice

Let's return to the venerated teacher of naturalist acting who unwittingly may have fueled the anti-intellectualism of her student by saying "You cannot think *and* do."

Surely his teacher did not intend her lesson to advocate against education, or against intellectual pursuits. She was, after all, following in the historical footsteps of Sanford Meisner, a venerated teacher of naturalism who claimed a lineage from Stanislavsky. She was practicing historical transmission, and tracking a long history of tension between thinking, feeling, and doing.

> **Student:** I'm getting the feeling: Don't think – do!
>
> **Meisner:** That's a very good feeling. That's an actor thinking. How does an actor think? He doesn't think – he does!

Student: Right.

Meisner: That's a good feeling.

(Longwell and Meisner 1987: 57)

For Meisner, doing is feeling, and feeling is in some distinction to thinking. Or rather, the way an actor thinks is to feel — "That's an actor thinking." Feeling, then, is a kind of thinking — but in the next sentence, no! "An actor doesn't think — he does!" But doing is "a good feeling." And feeling is ... "an actor thinking." The ground beneath thinking, feeling, and doing is cracked and slippery in Meisner, who was adapting (and has often been accused of reducing) the teachings of Stanislavsky (Krasner 2000).

In *An Actor Prepares*, Stanislavsky cites the teacher of his own teacher, the actor Mikhail Shchepkin, whom many regard as the father of psychological acting. As Stanislavsky tells his own students in *An Actor Prepares*, Shchepkin invested in a distinction between an actor of reason and an actor of feeling. But be careful! "Thinking" is not the opposite, here, of doing or feeling, nor feeling the opposite of "logic."

> "You may play well or you may play badly; the important thing is that you should play truly," wrote Shchepkin to his pupil Shumski. "To play truly means to be right, logical, coherent, to think, strive, feel and act in unison with your role." (Stanislavski 1989: 15)

The distinction is not between mind and body or thought and deed, but between playing truly and playing falsely, as if Shchepkin wanted, like Rousseau before him, to banish artificiality from the art form (though Rousseau, despite his own playwriting, would have just banished the art form itself). Here "true" indicates some kind of unison with the "facts" or "given circumstances" (Stanislavsky's words) of the role. In this way, Meisner's aphorism "Don't think – do!" might alter Stanislavsky significantly.[13] Consider this from Stanislavsky:

> "Well, what do you think?" asked the Director. "Can one sit on a chair, and for no reason at all be jealous? Or all stirred up? Or sad? Of course it is impossible. Fix this for all time in your memories: *On the stage there cannot be, under any circumstances, action which is directed immediately at the arousing of feeling for its own sake.* To ignore this rule results only in the most disgusting artificiality. *When you are choosing some bit of action leave feeling and spiritual content alone.* Never seek to be jealous, or to make love, or to suffer, for its own sake. *All such feelings are the result of something that has gone before. Of the thing that goes before you should think as hard as you can. As for the result, it will produce itself.* The false acting of passions, or of types, or the mere use of conventional gestures, – these are all frequent

faults in our profession. But you must get away from these unrealities. You must not copy passions or copy types. You must live in the passions and in the types. Your acting of them must grow out of your living in them." (1989: 42, emphasis in original)

False acting is also a kind of doing without thinking – it is a doing of "disgusting artificiality." Doing for its own sake is like feeling for its own sake, and just the kind of acting Stanislavsky abjured. For him, copies, imitations, replicas are not the "living" art, for acting, paradoxically, must be resolutely tied, in his system, to some idea of the past – "what came before" – in order to be "living."[14] Here, Stanislavsky actually advocates for thinking as an antidote to the grain of rote imitation, even rote "doing." The devil, here, is rote – not thought. To avoid "feeling for its own sake," which is feeling divorced from some kind of "reason," Stanislavsky advocates something that begins to look like historical thought: "Of the thing that goes before you should think as hard as you can." But make no mistake, this is not to think your own thoughts, but to "think as hard as you can" the thoughts demanded by the (theatrical, and often historical) situation.

It is interesting to consider linking Stanislavsky to such philosophers of history as R. G. Collingwood, who conceptualized thinking historical thoughts through situated reenactment. Writing his theories of historical reenactment in Britain in the 1920s and 1930s, Collingwood, like

Stanislavsky, was against "copying" but interested in repetition as a link to verity. Events that occurred in the past, writes Collingwood,

> can be historically known not by anything in the least analogous to perception, observation, or any process or act intelligibly describable as "apprehension", but by their *reenactment* in the mind of the historian. (1994: 449, emphasis added)

Collingwood goes on to assert that he is interested not in copies or replicas, but in the thing (here thought) itself. Because the past does not exist "as past," it cannot be copied: "How could anyone make a copy of something that does not exist?" he asks. Instead, he argues,

> The reenactment of the past in the present is the past itself so far as that is knowable to the historian. We understand what Newton thought by thinking — not *copies* of his thoughts — a silly and meaningless phrase — but his thought themselves over again. When we have done that, we know what Newton thought, not mediately, but immediately. (1994: 450, emphasis in original)

It is "the act of thought" that Collingwood is after.

> The historian's thought, then, neither is nor contains nor involves any copy of its object. The historian's thought is, or rather contains as one

of its elements, that object itself, namely the *act of thought* which the historian is trying to understand, re-thought in the present by himself. A person who failed to realize that thoughts are not private property might say that it is not Newton's thought that I understand, but only my own. That would be silly because, whatever subjective idealism may pretend, thought is always and everywhere *de jure* common property, and is *de facto* common property wherever people at large have the intelligence to think in common. (1994: 450, emphasis added)

However, unlike Stanislavsky, Collingwood was not at all invested in feeling – quite the contrary. Unlike Stanislavsky, Collingwood was decidedly against affect (Lamb 2008: 247). As we will see in the next section, it is *feeling* that can trouble an historian's imperative that might read something like: "Don't feel – think!"

We should turn, at this point, to Joseph Roach's important book *The Player's Passion* (1993). Roach charts a considerably long back-story to the tension we've been discussing between thinking, feeling, and doing in the history of theatre, which he reads in tandem with the history of science. Though he focuses his energy on the eighteenth century and Denis Diderot's then paradigmatic 1773 *The Paradox of the Actor*, Roach casts lines of tangled relation to the ancients as well as to today (when Stanislavsky seems to have replaced Diderot as paradigm). Telling the story of unresolved and ever re-boiling tensions about passions or feelings and theatricality in relationship to historically specific scientific attitudes to the body and the body's protean relationship to "truth," Roach argues, forcefully, that the "time-honored philosophical and scientific issue of the relationship of mind and body [...] underlies crucial questions of daily professional significance to the actor" (1993: 12–13). For Roach, contemporary questions of the proper routes of access to (or from) emotion are not easily divorced from precedence, nor simplistically situated in an uncomplicated "now" of performance that disappears at each contingent articulation. Roach vehemently cautions theatre historians against the habit of reading the long and varied history of theatre's negotiations with passions, emotions, reason, and ideas only "in relationship to the degree to which they anticipated Stanislavski" (1993: 15). For the question of emotion, he writes, "tends to defy settled conclusions" (1993: 11).

But let *The Player's Passion*, and Roach's *Cities of the Dead* (1996) as well, be required reading for any serious student of our topic. For now, let's return to the paradigm of Stanislavsky and his bid to have his actors, as historian Sharon Carnicke tells us, "play the cause not the effect" (2000: 26). Essentially Stanislavsky called for an actor to be in the *time* of the action, and whether the time of the action is set in the past or in the future, the time is to be "now" for the naturalist actor – not a copy of now. Both now, then – and then, now. His system is brimful of ways to access one time in another time, newly each time, or to enclose one time within another like a "circle of attention" that forms a kind of scrim between the time of the audience and the time of the actor's concentration (Stanislavski 1989: 89). Thus, as Stein eloquently noted in *Lectures in America*, the time of theatre is not necessarily the same time as the time of the audience (1935: 94). The actor's "now" is not the audience's "now," even as these "now"s and "then"s meet and bleed, paradoxically, into a shared moment. Theatre takes place in what Stein termed "syncopated time" (and her interest in and "nervousness" about syncopated time led her far away from the impulse to naturalism). In any case, for Stanislavsky, "thinking as hard as you can" – which is *not* the opposite of feeling but its onstage emissary – enables what might be called a temporal slip, or crack, in any number of directions.

Recall what we earlier said might be "simple" in our conjunction linking theatre and history: that theatre is an art of time and that time is the stuff of the stage. Theatre often makes itself in the "again, and again, and again" that is preparation, or re-performance. A lot of that preparation went on well before *you* entered to strut and fret upon the boards. Yes, you might know not to say the name of the *M* play, and you might not really need to know why, but when you are cast in *Macbeth* and begin to work with iambic pentameter and structures of the aside you will feel history rushing in at your very pores. You will be *in* history, as well as *of* it. Having thought about it, even cursorily, will lend gravity to your actions, will enable you to ride the brim of time with confidence, to feel it bend and stretch as the powerful living animal that, through you, it is.

It's no small matter this "history." The hauntedness of the stage – to invoke theatre historian Marvin Carlson (2001) – all the actors and directors and designers and playwrights and dramaturgs and theorists who worked as excavation artists before you – is bigger than you, and you had better be prepared to meet it. It will, like it or not, come to meet you.

Theatre and the historian

If the tension in theatre practice is sometimes between thinking and feeling, or thinking and doing, the same tension, turned inside out like a glove, can present itself to the historian, as we have already begun to suggest by thinking about Collingwood. And while there are as many methods to historiography as there are "ism"s in theatre, and while the history of history is studded with reorientations, there, too, thinking, doing, and feeling can be in tense and complicated interplay with each other. The place of feeling, or affective engagement, in historiography has been vexed. Though the long and sometimes embattled family relations between history and rhetoric in the discipline make far too large a dramatic tale to tell here (see LaCapra 1985), students often come to the seminar table today already well versed in the problem of the hoped-for "objective" or dispassionate fact.

The twentieth-century "linguistic turn" launched famous challenges that most contemporary students of history will recognize. Historical discourse, writes Michel de Certeau,

> gives itself credibility in the name of the reality which it is supposed to represent, but this authorized appearance of the "real" serves precisely to camouflage the practice which in fact determines it. Representation thus disguises the praxis that organizes it. (1986: 203)

That "disguise" (a deeply theatrical term) is rhetoric — modes of writing, speaking, narrativizing, and, basically, communicating.[15] Postmodern scholars like Roland Barthes and Hayden White returned history from science to mythology, asserting that historiography is a form of fiction. White, in particular, argued that there is no difference between form and content in historical writing:

> historical narratives are verbal fictions, the contents of which are as much *invented* as *found* and the forms of which have more in common with their counterparts in literature than they have with those in sciences. (1978: 82; see also Barthes 1981)

But literature — even fiction — is not theatre. So why study *theatre's* histories?

It is somewhat commonplace to acknowledge what Aristotle acknowledged in *The Poetics*, that as people we compose an understanding of ourselves, even learn to be human, through mimetic and representational practices (1987: 34). This is what medievalist Jody Enders, cited later in this book, will term "inherently mimetic propensities of human beings" (2005: xxvii). Though mimesis, in the history of the West at least, almost always gets a bad rap (a rap that Jonas Barish termed "the antitheatrical prejudice," as we explored above), it can hardly be ignored.[16] We've already recognized that language itself is a matter of reiteration, reuse. And we've already seen that even theatre – the form most associated with mimesis historically – contains as many diatribes against "copying" or "disgusting artificiality" as it does investments in "style" or celebrations of artifice as the height of the form.[17] Looking at representational practices – indeed looking at the myriad "disguises" in which the "real" circulates – can be, as Clifford Geertz wrote from an anthropological perspective, a way of looking at how and what people "tell themselves about themselves" (or, historically, told themselves about themselves) (1977: 448).

Geertz wanted to be able to read live performance practices as embodied "texts" that we could read *as if* documents, to understand ritual, theatre, and everyday modes of performance as repetitive acts engaged in collective "self-fashioning" – to borrow a phrase from literary historian Stephen Greenblatt (1980). But the flipside is equally important – "texts" can also always be understood as performance practices. Texts are not only residue but also continuance of sociocultural behavior. To access text we engage in – we perform – such actions as reading, writing, teaching, telling, and even, with Collingwood, "acts of thought" (1994: 450). Whether you are sitting at your desk, in your armchair, or in the archive or library itself, any text or material is

encountered "live," so to speak, in time. As historians excavate the traces of times before now, close attention to liveness,
to live practices, and to live modes of access (what behaviors
are permissible in archives, for example) can inform what we
make of what we encounter. Add to this the curious fact that
liveness is a quality that can jump across time as well as space
and questions proliferate. The jumpiness of liveness requires
not only a scholar's attention to texts, objects, and material
remains and not only a spectator's attentiveness to stories,
but an actor's or dancer's attentiveness to embodied engagement and the more immaterial (yet remaining or recurring)
substance of affect or feeling. Encounters with affect and the
transmission of affect are the historian's as well as the actor's
trade. Affect lodges in objects, in sentences, in architectures
and images as much as in and between living people, and
material can "come alive again" in an archive as well as on
stage. Ask any practiced archivist! Affect, and the liveness it
seems to root around in, are thus the purview not only of the
theatre maker, whose traffic in feelings crosses boundaries
between stage and house, but of any encounter crossing the
liminal borders separating a then from a now.

And perhaps it is not only the curious ways material can
seem to come alive in archives, or people from the long
past can appear *as if* alive in theatres, but also the ways
that residues of other times, including affective residues,
cross temporal boundaries as we touch things, persons,
events that are no longer entirely "here." For why is it only
the dead that appear to come alive? Do not the living also
cross a kind of threshold away from the strictly immediate

present moment? Liveness may not be the only door opened by affect in the passageways between then and now, as I have written about using the word "inter(in)animate" in *Performing Remains* (2011: 7). That is, just as theatre may not be entirely real, so too it may not be entirely, or only, live. A repeated gesture, an aged object, a clichéd phrase, an old letter, a footprint, a way of walking – all of these things, material and immaterial, might drag something of the no longer now, the no longer live, into the present, or drag the present into the no longer now.

The problem with passions

As perhaps my somewhat creepy preceding paragraph suggests, traffic in affect can present a trouble spot for reasonable historians as they encounter theatricality. Especially if time is considered to be only and entirely linear – moving in a "forward" direction that leaves the past behind. Theatre, playing so often in the space of "again," troubles linearity with repetition. Add to this that theatre is often considered (often falsely) to be aligned more with feelings than with ideas, and troubles escalate. Though the identification of theatre singularly with feelings, as we have seen with Meisner, is arguably an overemphasized association at best, it is the case that the engagement of the live body – the presence of the body as medium if you will – lends credence to this association. The live body, shot through with the present and susceptible to emotion, is – we are habituated to think – unreliable as purveyor of anything other than medical fact. So, too, the fleetingly live – the moment that appears to vanish into the next

moment — is like the fleetingness of feelings if looked at simplistically. The present disappears, as do feelings — right? But
of course the theatre also illustrates how the live recurs night
after night (the furthest thing from disappearance) and feelings remain … to be produced again, to be assembled again,
to be felt again the next night. Indeed, theatre can be called,
with Nicholas Ridout, an "affect machine" by which the faux
and the real copulate to produce a hybrid that might escape,
or at least combine, the delimiting conditions of both (2006:
168). Such hybrids can complicate any desire for accurate
and authentic historical truths, while simultaneously hinting
at the historical truth of inauthenticity.

Let's look at the problem this way. If affect is not a material remain, but an immaterial residue at best — a sensation — how can it be in any way trustworthy as "evidence"?
We are well versed in the following: something happening
in theatre or in a reenactment is not something *really* happening, even if the emotions that are produced in an audience, an actor, or any other participant are *real* emotions,
real sensations. Next comes the question of whether emotions are ever simply real, or, as psychoanalysis instructs,
often screens for unconscious processes that mask a temporal remove. Emotions, laced with other times, and perhaps even borne in the porous nature of time itself, cannot
be trusted. Time moves forward — right? And emotion? At
best, emotion steers a wobbly course bleeding time and
space indiscriminately. Already the ground is buckling
beneath us the minute we try to take feeling as fact. Though
of course feelings happen, and thus are facts, they appear

to refuse to remain for the archive in the way an object or a document or a material artifact remains, and so, like performance itself, we assume they cannot be controlled, or harnessed, as reliable. At least, this is our common or simplistic approach to the matter of immaterial remains.

In the theatre at least, if not also in everyday life, emotions or feelings or even thoughts are displaced off of a *real* event to take place in a time that is not strictly delimitable to "now" or to "then." Anyone who has grieved for any length of time or smiled at a picture of a loved one knows the survival, even preservationist aspects of feelings – and yet feelings cannot be preserved, we assume. A thought, thought again, is still a thought – even, with Collingwood, *the* historical thought. If music, played again, is still the piece of music played (not a debauched or false copy of the music) and if writing, read again, is still the trace of the author's time, why would a feeling, accessed across time, or felt *again*, not also bear something of a historical trace? Is displacement necessarily falseness? Or is displacement, or syncopation, actually a mode – *the* mode – of access, of communication, of experience, of, in fact, any record?

If displacement is a given, and not the problem itself, why is it emotion that is the problem? Why do we consider emotion so untrustworthy? Why do we say you can get dangerously swept up by emotions, and not dangerously swept up by ideas (as if emotion and idea were completely separable)? Let's continue with this problem for a moment longer. A written record existing in an archive is displaced off of a real event, and even an historical artifact is displaced simply by time, and yet records and artifacts can stand as evidence, as aspects of one time preserved in another time. But feelings? Thoughts? Gestures? Stances? How can feelings be evidence? How can a live body be a trace? We are habituated to the following: footprints are traces – not living feet themselves! Aren't feelings the private property of the self-possessed individual and not something sharable in time or across space, at a physical remove? If feelings are "private" property, are they nontransferable, nonexchangeable? But of course they are exchangeable: aren't feelings in fact for sale in the theatre – that is, precisely a matter of exchange? So, more to the point of the problem: aren't feelings misleading, sentimental, and womanish personal investment, dragging us far afield of "hard, cold fact" (Berlant 2008)? Aren't feelings *fakable*? And *therefore* untrustworthy? This begins to look like the antitheatricality issue all over again. How can you trust your private feelings? But if feelings are exchangeable, are they really *only* private? Only personal? Are they not also, inherently, political? Whose feelings, where, when, and how, are accounted reliable? And again, how do we parse the fake – the manipulated and produced feeling – from something we still imagine to be "accurate" or "authentic"?

Surely, something pretending to be "then," or posturing in the subjunctive "as if" of theatre, is not *really* then, even if you imagine that it might *feel* like then. The "as if" of theatre and reenactment is neither the "is" nor the "was." Even if "real" things are employed in theatre – props can be real things but they are also "merely" props, reassigned to the faux by virtue of the theatrical frame (Sofer

2003) – and even if "real" emotions or thoughts seem to result from the manipulation of things and bodies on stage, these all appear to service the ultimate "not real" of the theatre. It would be fine if we could just leave it there, and never allow the real and not real to cohabitate. But the reality is that the not real is often – very often – not far behind, or far ahead, or very far to the side of the real. They track in tandem, they syncopate and copulate, like the wily ampersand of our title. As Bert O. States has written: "What happens, *when* it happens, in the theatre, is, as Shakespeare's Polixenes might say, art. But the art itself is nature" (1987: 47).

The theatre is one site where the fake can produce the real and the real colludes in the construction of the fake. This is precisely why it is interesting for us, even essential for us, to think deeply and rigorously about theatre's role, its participation, its essential imbrication in and as history, in and as everyday life. But if the tangle of the faux and the real, and the manipulation of our uncertainty, is part of the "magic," even the "enchantment" of the stage, the historian aims to separate fact from shrouds of feelings that may be said to obscure access to *what actually took place*. Though it would be hard, if not impossible, to find an event that did not result from, involve, or trigger human registers of emotion, don't we want to separate feelings from fact? And yet both in the theatre (which does not want to be real at the end of the day, even when it wants to be, with Stanislavsky, "living") and in history (where the real is the aim of account), understanding emotions is vital. Understanding the causes and effects of feelings and thinkings and doings is as much the craft of the actor as it is of the historian, if from differing directions. Theatricality rarely sticks to the confines of the playhouse, after all, but, slippery or "void" as it may be, composes "all the world."

Nevertheless, concerns about the ways in which feelings can infect our access to what *really* happened in the past are appropriate concerns. And simply because history, as a written account, must traffic in fiction or in disguise (if we agree even partially with White or de Certeau), it does not follow that what happened "then" was fiction, or that the fictions that may slip into any telling about the past completely overtake the register of remains. Surely a document such as a letter written to a loved one from a battlefield is closer to what happened on that battlefield than any *contemporary* feeling that might be provoked by the letter read at a temporal remove? And reenactment? Any feeling evoked from reenacting the writing of a letter while pretending to be a soldier at a hundred-year, or a thousand-year remove – that feeling is suspect at best. Feelings change, right? The document remains the same? The document belongs to the past, whereas feelings belong only to the present moment of the person experiencing feelings, right? And where there are no documents, but only an empty field – standing in that field is not standing with one's life at stake with gunfire, and real bullets, aimed at one's head! Dying on the field is not the same as lying down and pretending to bloat in the sun – surely! And sitting in a theatre watching an actor pretending to stand or to fall on a battlefield... all of these are *different* from "what really happened."

Few would claim that reenactment, like any historical account, is not composed in difference from the thing itself. But when, why, and how is "difference," like displacement, entirely debilitating? Can difference be manipulated to produce *anything* viable in the realm of sensation or affect that might stand as some kind of evidence, some kind of residue, some kind of remain? Is difference always only wrong?

In "Historical Reenactment, Extremity, and Passion," literary historian Jonathan Lamb includes theatre as a form of historical reenactment and historical reenactment as a form of theatre, and following historians such as Benedetto Croce and R. G. Collingwood, he seeks to "reconcile" cognitive impartiality (assumed for history) and affective investment (assumed for theatre and reenactment) (2008: 240). In his introduction to the collection *Settlers, Creoles, and Historical Reenactment*, Lamb boils the relationship between historical actuality and live reenactment down to the following: "the passions of reenactment become very intense indeed, and instead of possessing the past we are possessed by it" (2010: 1). This becoming possessed versus taking possession demands caution, though it does seem to have its uses for Lamb – particularly that reenactment allows our senses, if not our minds, to be "alert to the mystery of regeneration and the reappearance of what had been supposed to have gone forever" (2010: 17). In short, for Lamb the question of "passions" and "possession" troubles the dispassionate or "non-affective" aims of proper history, but its impropriety can be "regenerative" – if only of "mystery." Lamb, who has himself participated in reenactment, is more familiar with this "mystery" – and more "sympathetic" to it – than many. But we might ask: What is appropriate and supposedly non-mysterious about possessing something, but inappropriate and mysterious about being possessed?

Writing history, it seems for Lamb, is a mode of pos-sessing something from the past, but reenacting is a mode of being or becoming possessed by affect or passion – in a word, feeling. And, for Lamb, as for our venerated teacher of acting discussed above, it is not possible to think *and* feel. Becoming possessed, versus possessing, seems, for Lamb, to threaten critical historical analysis – the realm of "idea." Lamb follows Baruch Spinoza to claim, again, that: "A mind operating under the influence of passion is in vain pursuit of an adequate idea" (2008: 246). But why are passion and affect, linked by Spinoza and Lamb to the body, not *adequate* in the pursuit of an idea? And who is to legislate the adequate from the inadequate, feeling from idea? There are worlds full of problems to unpack here, not unrelated to the slip and slide noted earlier in theatre's own vexed relationships to thinking, doing, and feeling – and many have been quite eloquent on the historical tracks of those problems. Again, Roach's *The Player's Passion* (1993) is a must-read in this regard, but so is Sam Wineburg's essay "Making Historical Sense" on modes of teaching his-tory. One high school student interviewed by Wineburg told him directly that what he had learned in his classes was that the best mind for historical analysis would have to be Vulcan – paradoxically a deeply theatrical reference to a character from the future known for his inability to feel (2000: 315). Though this Vulcan view is obviously obsolete for most contemporary historians, nevertheless, much like the obsolete antitheatricality Fischer-Lichte notes at the start of her *History of European Drama and Theatre* (2002), it carries on an active vestigial life in the trenches of the profession.

Thinking about embodied passions that can "possess" an historian (or an actor), versus a critical or reasoning mind that an historian (or actor) possesses, can quickly become related to geopolitics on a global scale. Let's return to Lamb's statement "the passions of reenactment become very intense indeed, and instead of possessing the past we are possessed by it." If we have been interpreting Lamb's use of the word "possession" to refer to spirit possession, possession trance, or other practices of mediumship, another sense of the word – ownership – seems to attend as well. For the "adequate" historian possesses the past, in Lamb's formation. And here Lamb does not seem to imply that the adequate historian haunts, or "rides," or "seizes," or "mounts" the past like a dead ancestor might visit or ride or seize the possessed, taking over the body of the past and speaking through it (Morris 2006: 22). Rather, Lamb's usage implies property – owning the past rather than being owned by it. But why is it better to own something – to take as property – than to be owned by something – to be spoken through or taken by? Is thinking on the (preferable) master's side, and feeling on the (undesirable) slave's side?

Thinking on the male side, and feeling on the female? As Roach pointed out, writing on the context of the flesh trade and its aftermath in *Cities of the Dead*:

> The ethos of spirit possession pointedly focuses attention on the autonomy and ownership of living bodies, an attention most unwelcome to slaveholders in antebellum times as well as to their heirs in the era of Jim Crow. (1996: 208)

This should remind us that cautioning against, if not legislating against, possession and its "passions" has its own history, and one deeply connected not only to cross-cultural modes of performance but to broader gendered[18] and geopolitical investments in appropriate, legitimate, or "adequate" modes of accessing, tracking, archiving, and accounting for the proper place of the so-called dead in the so-called past.

For who can "possess" the past as private property? And why does the jump of affect or passion in mimetic, embodied engagement threaten the drive to "authenticity and accuracy" that defines, as we saw above, historicity? In his chapter "The Circulation of Social Energy" in *Shakespearean Negotiations*, Greenblatt argues that mimesis is always a matter of exchange not conditioned by private property. I read him to suggest that while enabling the energy of exchange — between actors and audience or between past and present — mimesis is always potentially in resistance to one of the primary aspects of modernity's relations: the condition of private ownership.

I had dreamed of speaking with the dead, and even now I do not abandon this dream. But the mistake was to imagine that I would hear a *single* voice, the voice of the other. If I wanted to hear one, I had to hear the many voices of the dead. And if I wanted to hear the voice of the other, I had to hear my own voice. The speech of the dead, like my own speech, is not private property. (1989: 20)

This is to say that there may be more at stake than simply that collective memory and embodied transmission can confuse the disembodied historical "facts" of what happened, troubling the clarity of history with the cacophony of multiple perspectives and inadequate or error-ridden embodied recall.

The problem with archives

The "more" that is at stake is worth exploring. Diana Taylor has been eloquent on the geopolitics that historically aligned European colonizers with the archive and the "primitive" colonized with performance. Taylor's important book *The Archive and the Repertoire* (2003) takes us to the scene of encounter between European colonizers and the colonized in the Americas to explain how performance and orature in live modes of telling history were necessarily debased in direct relationship to the archiving of written records. Taylor makes clear the geopolitical systems of privilege in the scenario of conquest, by which documentation and preservation of text *as against performance* became imperial tools for the subjugation of colonized populations. It was important for the colonizers that live performance, oral traditions of transmission and embodied, performance-based ways of worlding[19] the past, would *not* remain as valid indicators of history. The tracks of embodied knowledge, and body-to-body transmission in ritual, theatre, dance, sport, song, and folklore, had to be debased in relationship to the official history given only to exist in document- and object-based archives – archives controlled by the colonizer (Thomas 1993; Stoller 2009). The body, that is, was not to be considered an adequate archive, and bodily ways of knowing were not to be acknowledged as knowledge. Performance was relegated to disappearance (Schneider 2011: 87–110). And here we can recall that "possession" would be a performance form associated with the religions of "primitive" peoples – those without history, as the philosopher G. W. F. Hegel would claim in the 1830s of Africa.[20]

Some may assume that we are well beyond the racist and gender-marked claims that have dis-privileged embodied modes of transmitting historical knowledge over time. But it is still the case that performance threatens the terms of captive or discrete, ownable, legitimated, and apparently dispassionate remains dictated by the archive. This is in part why the logic of the imperial archive – that utopic "operational field of projected total knowledge" (Thomas 1993: 11) – is still alive and well. Because oral history and its performance practices are always decidedly repeated in time, oral historical practices are always reconstructive, always incomplete, always inflected by difference. In performance, the pristine self-sameness of an "original," an artifact so valued by the archive, is rendered impossible. Though many have claimed that attitudes have shifted in favor of a "new" history that incorporates collective memory, performative practices, and "intangible heritage," that "new" history is manifested in the constitution of what historian Jacques Le Goff describes as "radically new kinds of archives, of which the most characteristic are oral archives" (1992: 95–96).[21] But note with care: the oral is not here approached as already an archive, a performance-based or embodied archive. Rather, oral histories are constituted anew, recorded and "saved" through technologies of recording in the name of identicality and materiality. Though this "new" archiving is supposedly preservative, why must the oral or intangible be recorded in order to be saved? And doesn't such saving fundamentally alter the *historical* nature of oral transmission that may not follow rules of property, possession, and ownership dictated by the archive – thus essentially altering or damaging the "record"? Why do we continue to assume that if performance-based practices are not given to documentation or sonic recording, or otherwise made tangible, visible, houseable within an official archive, they are irretrievably lost to history, disappeared? And when we acknowledge intangible cultural heritage, how are efforts to preserve still linked to imperial archival conditions that ultimately serve to legislate private property? Would someone engaged in intangible cultural heritage be an historian?

In that case would the performing historian *be* the record and the analyst at once?

I suggested above that someone performing in an historical play (and what pre-scripted play is not historical?) is clearly a theatre artist, but it is not clear that that performer is necessarily an historian, despite the constitutive againness of performance practices. What if a theatre or performance artist is explicitly performing "oral history"? Commonly, even if a theatre artist is telling stories about the past, even stories that were written down about the past, and even direct citations from oral historical documents, it does not necessarily follow that that actor is *also* an historian, or that the *performance* of oral transmission is itself a work of history. In *Doing Oral History*, Donald Ritchie makes this clear. He even makes it "simple" – though there is nothing simple about it:

> Simply put, oral history collects memories and personal commentaries of historical significance through *recorded* interviews. An oral history interview generally consists of a well-prepared interviewer questioning an interviewee and recording their exchange in audio or video format. (2003: 19, emphasis added)

By this account, oral history is not the embodied presentation itself. Transmitting an account orally is not, itself, oral history. Essential for an oral account to become history is some technological medium of recording *by an oral historian*. That is, the speaker/reciter is not already an historian by virtue of embodied speech. Ritchie makes it clear that recording is not embodied replay, but "audio or video." He goes on:

> Recordings of the interview are transcribed, summarized, or indexed and then *placed in a library or archives*. These interviews may be used for research or excerpted in a publication, radio or video documentary, museum exhibition, dramatization or other form of public presentation. Recordings, transcripts, catalogs, photographs and related documentary materials can also be posted on the Internet. (2003: 19, emphasis added)

This is to say that, at least for Ritchie, oral history can be used *in* theatre (dramatization), but oral history is not the dramatization, the rendering of live theatre, itself. Why is oral transmission "history" only if it is given as an object to "the library or archives"? Does someone engaged in telling an historical narrative cease to be an historian the minute she becomes a performer? Here, the body is clearly not already an archive, nor even a means of recording or preserving. Compare this view with that of Paul Zumthor, a medieval historian and linguist who wrote in *Oral Poetry* that not only is oral history always already theatre, but "Is not all literature fundamentally theatre?" (1990: 29). For Zumthor, the record is always relative to embodied reception, and embodied (re)iteration is already a record. If, as he claims, performative and theatrical activity are fundamental to all human communication then theatre and performance are essential ingredients in all efforts to communicate the past. In order to "introduce into the study of literature the concept of sensorial perception, or in other words, the living body," the idea of performance and physical engagement is essential (1990: 19).

But perhaps to say that everything is theatre (with Zumthor) is no more helpful to the problem of live reception in relation to the past than it is to claim (with Ritchie) that the historical record is *only* that which can be given to be housed, by technological reproduction, in a material archive. We are caught in a temporal conundrum, and trying to solve the puzzle by complete inclusion on the one hand or complete exclusion on the other does not helpfully further our understanding of what might be better approached as ambivalent and porous relations between then and now, or history and theatre, or thinking and feeling. For surely, not everything about the past can be accessed by the "living body," just as not everything about the past can be maintained in a material archive or technological record.[22]

It's starting to look as if the stickiest issue at the copulative conjunction "theatre and history" concerns the place of historical evidence in relation to the living body and its passions. The living body and its "possessions" appear to disrupt the ability of a record to be a purveyor of facts we can "possess." But if there is such a thing as embodied history that replays in the present, why would theatre not be a kind of living archaeology, or archaeology of the live? For now it's important to note that the notion of embodied history is, of course, quite an established idea, with a reach well beyond theatre practice – we've already mentioned orature (wa Thiong'o 2007) as well as Freud and Foucault, but think also of the efforts of feminist, queer, and race critical historians eager to retrieve the history of those who, by virtue of their bodies or bodily practices, were, as Sheila Rowbotham has written, "hidden from history" (1973). Bodies and history, that is, go way back as fraught bedfellows, with the evidence of acts and feelings undertaken by some bodies given more privileged space in the archive than the acts and feelings undertaken by other bodies. Theatre and dance, the embodied arts par excellence, would seem, then, prime places to explore what bodies nevertheless may have retained of knowledge, of stories, of modes of transmission alternate to or at least in addition to "libraries and archives."[23]

Studying performance practices on the stage and in everyday life, and their often extremely complex overlap in the making as well as in the telling of history's stories, can only aid in the challenges of thinking and feeling cross-temporally. If "theatre" and "history" are clearly not the same thing, or bear different relations to the constellation of thinking, doing, and feeling, they certainly do speak through and to each other. Understanding the variant languages of both can enrich each in its own domain. If, in theatre, thinking may not be the opposite of feeling but its emissary, so in history, feeling may not be the opposite of idea but its emissary.

Whose history is theatre's history?

We've discussed students of theatre arts and students of history, as if only those two might be interested in "theatre history." Before returning to the copulative "and" let's pause briefly over another question: Whose history is theatre's history? Does it belong only to theatre? In the 1980s Brenda Laurel wrote a book, brought out again in 2013 in a second edition, titled *Computers as Theatre*. She basically gives computers to the ancient Greek god of theatre, Dionysus, and likens the screenal architecture of computers to the proto-screenality of the Theatre of Dionysus at Athens. While there is precious little rigorous theatre history in Laurel's book, the suggestion is worth following through: the history of computers is *theatre history*. And the same can be argued, perhaps more obviously, for television, film, and even photography.

The prehistory of photography is theatre history because the backstory of the "still" predates the invention of chemicals of capture. An "interinanimation" of moving and still, flesh and stone, live and nonlive, as well as other copulative conjunctions we've been exploring as "theatrical," such as faux and real, is redolent across the arts wherever people participate in art, ritual, performance (Schneider 2011). For mimesis is not simple imitation, but a powerful movement of potential becoming, where sameness and difference cohabitate.

If we have defined "theatre" and "history," we have not yet paid attention to the term "mimesis," though "telling ourselves about ourselves," whether via theatre or historical narrative, or even nonrepresentational arts, necessarily involves mimesis. As Plato has Critias say in *Critias*: "Everything we say must surely be mimesis and image-making" (cited in Halliwell 2002: 37). Classicist Stephen Halliwell has argued forcefully that mimesis, from the ancient Greek μίμησις, is regularly poorly translated in its Latinized form of *imitatio*, or "imitation" (2002:13), and the depth in the concept is lost to surface notions of "mere" copying, linked, as the poor debased mime, with what Stanislavsky might term "disgusting artificiality." But for Plato, as for his student Aristotle, there is nothing "mere" about mimesis.[24] Mimesis, writes Halliwell, "can be construed as the use of an artistic medium (words, sounds, physical images) to signify and communicate certain hypothesized realities" – and not simply by virtue of imitating them along lines of visual verisimilitude (2002: 16).[25] To hypothesize is to lay down a proposition, a thesis, such as "This is happening now," or "This is what happened then," or even "This is a poem," or "This is a painting," or "This is a fact." The hypothesized "this" can occur via evocation, imitation, imaging, abstraction, lyricism, prose, poetry, drama, painting, nonrepresentational dance, etc. It is the problem of emotional, uncritical absorption in relation to the hypothesized real that continually provokes Plato's anxieties over mimesis. And as Halliwell convincingly argues, across his oeuvre Plato remained profoundly ambivalent about mimesis because of its power. "What is ultimately at stake [for Plato] is not the intrinsic nature of mimetic images but the use made of them and the basis of understanding on which that use rests" (2002: 59). Acting, for example, is never "only" acting, nor entertainment ever "mere" (thus, actors should take heart that Plato had the deepest respect if also the deepest fear for the power of their enterprise!). Neither is rhetoric simply false. Plato's ambivalence is not, in other words, dismissal – for Plato nowhere suggests that the question of mimesis and its powerful uses should not be fully, perhaps even endlessly, debated (2002: 39). And with that we might readily agree.

The power of mimesis is the power of exchange, by which a *real* response is crafted, provoked, or manipulated in an audience (much as a philosophical point can be crafted, provoked, or manipulated in Plato's own dialectical exchange). Mimesis becomes associated with motifs of "deception" or "persuasion" because the "persuasive vividness of a mimetic work or performance is more than the achievement of [imitation; it] involves the creation of something that, through its sense of *life*, can affect the viewer or hearer emotionally." It is a matter, Halliwell adds, "of the power to 'bewitch,' or 'enchant'" (2002: 21, emphasis in original). The ancients, Halliwell tells us, conceived of mimesis as the representation of a world in relation to which the audience occupies the position of an absorbed or engrossed "witness." In this way mimesis becomes the real through the vehicle of the thinking and feeling witness, even as that reality has been subject to the powers of representation. This becoming real is powerful. Thus it is the *uses* of representation, by whom and to what ends, that concerns Plato.

But our question is about whose history is theatre's history. Interestingly, debates about mimesis at the basis of philosophy grew in intensity at a moment relatively coterminous, in the West, with the "births" of theatre and history. The "father of history" is a title generally conferred upon Herodotus, though he has also been called the "father of lies" (Evans 1968; Hartog 1988: xix). Either way, Herodotus, author of *Histories*, is credited with attempting to collect evidence systematically, either by hearsay (thus his fathering of lies) or by eyewitness account (thus his fathering of history), and arranging his evidence in narrative form which he would then recite before a live audience. But what is interesting for us here is the coincidence of multiple births – in triplicate – "theatre," "history," and "philosophy." The triumvirate are still umbilically related, and their trajectory profoundly shared, even if, more often than not, their fundamental interrelation is obfuscated by our post-Enlightenment investment in discrete disciplinarity.[26]

Let's return to the arts and the question of theatre history. As the Roman-era statuary lining the Theatre of Dionysus continue to intone: The live takes place in the presence of the still and the still takes place live. Tableaux vivants, and the "pose" that constructs the photograph, reach back beyond the camera to ask more fundamental questions than questions about mechanical apparatuses. A pose – a moment of a frozen image, a hand raised, perhaps, as a hail – freezes time even if only for a fraction of a second, and drags another moment into a "betweeness" where a performer and a spectator participate in temporal manipulation. If hands were raised to hail in ages far predating the present, how is the gesture of the raised hand not itself a kind of historical residue? How is gesture, such as the raised hand, not also an "object" that can be studied as evidence of continuity (continuity composed through repetition)?

Thinking of photography again, if the notion of an imprint can be seen in the "negative" hands on cave walls imprinted in the ice age throughout the south of France and the north of Spain (and indeed around the world),[27] how is photography's prehistory not in fact older than the nineteenth-century invention of the "camera"? And how does that history (of photography) not then share something profound with the history of gesture, which also predates theatre proper? In fact, Kaja Silverman gives the ice age caves to the prehistory of cinema, writing that "ever since the inception of cave drawing, it is via images that we see and are seen" (1996: 195). Silverman asserts that given the human faculty of image-making, we are always removed or alienated from ourselves, separated from the "directly lived" via the visual worlds we make – and have been so, via "specularity," at least since the ice age. But Richard Schechner, who gives the caves to a prehistory of theatre, does not allow specularity to imply remove. He claims Paleolithic art for interactive performance, or embodied ritual, writing that some cave art was ritually rubbed and touched, stroked or otherwise tactilely fondled by participants who might not neatly fall under the rubric of "spectator" (1998: 69–70). But my point here is that either way, either standing at a remove to view or touching and handling with intimate contact, live human bodies interacted with stone, image, gesture, art *then* as well as *now*. Evidence is not only, never only, the object or image at a remove, but the very hands or torsos or eyeballs that come into contact with the object, text, artifact, or gesture ... now. The now of our encounter is certainly different from the then (we may not know what the handprints meant to ice age participants), but it is not *only* different. The body in relation is, despite radically shifting contexts, in relation *again*. And given that cave art witnessed human rituals (even rituals of "specularity") for thousands of years, even the most ancient of encounters would have been, also, encounters *again*. Againness, then, is *also* a matter for historical thought, and not only the supposedly debauched terrain of the fake and false "theatre."

Thus theatre's history may share the history of other arts. But students of theatre history are very aware that their area of study does not produce remains in the same way that other arts, such as painting or sculpture or even negative hands on cave walls, generate objects or images that remain as materials to study over time. One can go to a museum, for instance, and stand before a painting made decades, centuries, millennia before the present. But can one "go" to ancient Greece to study the theatre of 240 BCE? Well, yes, one can go to the ruins of the Theatre of Dionysus in Athens and there encounter remnants of the architecture of production – but is the architecture *the* performance? Just because a proscenium arch is related, historically, to Roman triumphal arches doesn't mean that we claim live performance that happens within the arch today to be *Roman* history. And yet, clearly, as with the tracks of rhetoric, we *might* acknowledge a porous kind of transmission by which live and stone or wooden structure complicatedly repeat a shared past. So, too, with hands raised in hail. Something is remembered, even if a great deal is also, and simultaneously, forgotten. If we habitually make solid distinctions between object remains and live enactment, we may too often forget to ask what forgetting might remember (more on forgetting anon).

While it is certainly true that live performance appears, unlike object remains, to "disappear," it does no good as theatre historians either to sit on our hands or to throw them up and stop there. Hand to hand, theatre has nevertheless persisted, endured, changing shape over time in infinite variety, and so something of the "live" as remainder insists upon account. In fact, we might look at theatre as a kind of liveness that remains. For if performance disappears, it also, and quite consistently, reappears. The gap between disappearance and reappearance may not be as entirely untrustworthy as we are habituated to assume, and it may not be enough to say: What happened once is not the same as what happens again. For what happens once is also not necessarily *entirely* different either. In the seeming gap between sameness and difference, something of theatre takes shape as historical. And something of historicity takes place as gestural, postural, live, and, yes, theatrical.

The gap between one instance in the theatre and the next, like one night before one audience and the next night before another audience, is a constitutive gap at the heart of the art form itself. As we have discussed, theatre is constituted in repetition. Not only the repetitions from one performance to the next, and from one production to the next, but the very nature of acting "as if" manipulates a gap between a thing, person, or place and that which performs as surrogate. The gap is at once temporal (a script usually predates a performance) and constitutional (the playing of the gap, in the gap, is what theatre does). Thus theatre can be called an art of time, and also an art of passage – the passing of one person, thing, or idea into another person, thing, or idea where person, thing, and idea are *in play*. Such playing at the gap is a kind of becoming, even if momentary. Paradoxically, the gap of difference is what is the same in the art form over time – and thus difference is a kind of sameness basic to the theatre. To chart the differences would be one approach to theatre's histories (a theatre historian might recount how the 1898 *Seagull* was *different* from today's *Seagull* in such and such ways, or even catalog the more minor but inevitable differences in a production night to night). But to account for *sameness* involves engaging in a riddle by which "disappearance" and "difference" are, paradoxically, what remain the same. To play it differently would be, to some extent, to play it the same as it had previously been played when previously live: in difference.

We are awash in paradox. Or scrambling about in the Minotaur's labyrinth without Ariadne's thread! The slippery copulation of sameness *and* difference here has returned us to the rascally ampersand, and paradox seems to meet us in any direction we turn at this crossroads between theatre and history. For if we have established anything in all of our prior sections, it is only that theatre and history are both: the same and different. It is as if they are coming to the question of "What happened?" from opposite corners of the earth to meet in the vexed and overlapping middle. Entirely suspicious of each other, and blinking at each other through competing approaches to the question of what constitutes an archive, they have forgotten their umbilical ties, shared DNA, mimetic symbiosis. We might here do well only to recall that their difference is the result of their sameness, their sameness the result of their difference.

On knives and blood

To return to the copulative ampersand in our title *Theatre & History*, we have seen throughout this small book that other troubling copulations attend the spaces between the theatrical and the historical. Most profound may be the fake and the real, the remembered and the forgotten, the live and the dead. We will think together about each of them in this final section – though they, too, will overlap and oscillate each among the others.

The alignment of theatre with fakery runs deep in habits of antitheatricality within the art world at large, but also, as Stanislavsky's condemnation of "disgusting artificiality" exemplifies, within theatre itself. The stance against artificiality can make for some strange bedfellows. Who, for example, would put twenty-first-century intermedia performance artists in bed with Stanislavsky? Or in bed with Wineburg's student's Vulcan variety of historian? Yet many today consider "live art" or "performance art" to be the domain of the "real," in opposition to "disgusting artificiality" or staginess, and this prompts some contemporary performance practitioners to argue for a deep distinction between performance art or live art and theatre, despite the fact that both take place live, in time, and often on stages or platforms or other areas demarcated for performers and audiences, and despite theatre's own historical push against convention.[28] Performance artist Marina Abramović is the most recent famous antitheatricalist in this regard:

> To be a performance artist, you have to hate thea-
> tre. Theatre is fake: there is a black box, you pay
> for a ticket, and you sit in the dark and see some-
> body playing somebody else's life. The knife is
> not real, the blood is not real, and the emotions
> are not real. Performance is just the opposite:
> the knife is real, the blood is real, and the emo-
> tions are real. It's a very different concept. It's
> about true reality. (Cited in O'Hagan 2010)

For Abramović, true reality is opposed to fake reality as well as, perhaps, true falsity – whatever such word combinations may mean. At the end of the day, it is simple for Abramović: theatre is fake and live art performance is real. But how do we "really" parse the fake and the real? Policing real emotions and fake emotions is famously unreliable, in everyday life as well as on theatrical stages. Just ask anyone who has ever argued with a loved one, or cried at a movie, or been pumped up by cheerleaders or carried along by a crowd! (The question of parsing becomes even thornier in terms of the transmission of "historical emotion," as feelings may travel in time through repetition via the gap between real and faux.) Knives and blood, however, Abramović's other indicators, may do the trick. For, surely, there is a difference between real blood and stage blood, just as there is between real death and fake death — and the difference, surely, matters. But even here, at least historically speaking, the fake and the real, like the live and the dead, can be notoriously difficult to completely sever.

Since a play like *The Seagull* doesn't pretend to be about "real" historical events, let's choose a history play, which we can define, with Tom Stern, as a play with "focused, engaged depiction of real events, which assume responsible engagement with the sources on the part of the playwright and independent, historical knowledge on the part of the spectator" (2013: 81). Let's think, as Stern does, about Shakespeare's history play *Julius Caesar* for a moment. This play, indebted to historical sources, recounts several famous historical deaths. The first is Caesar's, killed at the hand of conspirators, including his close friend the Roman praetor Marcus Brutus. The last death is Brutus's as he commits suicide by running onto his own sword. These "deaths," replayed in the theatre, are not "real." We applaud the actors afterwards for performances well delivered and assume they will go on to die again the next night on stage, live. But the rhetoric that they deliver on stage — how "real" is that? We can parse the historical Brutus and the historical Caesar from their theatrical afterlives easily as concerns knives and blood, but less easily as concerns rhetoric.

"We know we are in Rome as we watch *Julius Caesar* because everyone is talking Roman — Roman oratory and rhetoric about Roman virtue and power," writes Garry

Wills in *Rome and Rhetoric*. "Of course," Wills goes on, "all of Shakespeare is highly rhetorical." Shakespeare's education would have been an education in Roman rhetoric — more textbooks of rhetoric were produced in that period than in any other, so to study Renaissance England would be at least in part to study Rome, or to study "the way Elizabethan schoolboys were taught that Romans had spoken" (2011: 37–38). To study, that is, contemporary translations of Cicero and the transmission of history in the rhetorical exercises of schoolchildren. To study Elizabethan England would be, in part, to study the way Rome had been passed down in history as history. And much of that history is theatre history.

Figures of rhetoric delivered on stage are not fake rhetoric — they are, simply, rhetoric. And *something* of Rome is transmitted orally, but what value is oral transmission or habits and conventions of rhetoric to history? To what degree can live rhetoric, or ways of speaking and gesturing, of posing and posturing, aid the effort to determine "what happened" or "what is happening"? We have already looked at this, cursorily, as concerns orature. For now, consider that figures of speech may not be "real knives" or "real blood" but are real ways of speaking — ways of speaking laced with complicated overlays of history: Roman, Elizabethan, and ...

It was the very "real" historical actor become US president, Ronald Reagan, who quoted Shakespeare's *Julius Caesar* in a speech titled "Creators of the Future" on March 8, 1985:

> I believe we conservatives have captured the moment, captured the imagination of the

American people. And what now? [...] You
remember your Shakespeare: "There is a tide in
the affairs of men which, taken at the flood, leads
on to fortune. Omitted, all the voyage of their
life is bound in shallows and in miseries. On such
a full sea are we now afloat. And we must take
the current when it serves, or lose our ventures."
I spoke in the — [applause]. It's typical, isn't it?
I just quoted a great writer, but as an actor, I
get the bow. [Laughter]. (Cited in Critchlow and
MacLean 2009: 112)

There is no blood and no knife here to help us parse the
theatrical from the real. Reagan claims a political tide by
recalling a theatrical tide that itself is recalling an historical tide, and at least in Reagan's case, the politician then
acknowledges his performance *as an actor* – to laughter. Of
course, Reagan had literally, historically, been a professional
actor, and while surely that bit of theatre history matters,
the history of politics is studded with the theatrical power of
rhetoric. Where no "real" "actor" stands behind the mask, is
the deployment of theatricality nevertheless *real*? Here "theatrical" does not so much mean "fake" as it means composed
in the manipulations and reiterations of language and gesture
in a "theatre," or arena, of action. Such theatricality can have
profound cross-temporal reality effects.[29] "You remember
your Shakespeare," Reagan begins, and then proceeds to
quote the character Brutus, who, *if* anyone remembers their
Shakespeare, delivers this speech on seizing the moment to

commit assassination in the midst of a play that will, if anything, render that very action deeply ill fated and ill advised. Brutus does not get what he wants, and it is arguably rhetoric (Anthony's) that proves the more powerful weapon upon the "real" than any knife or any blood.

Indeed, remembering Shakespeare's play, as well as remembering what became of Brutus historically, seems vital in trying to understand Regan's paradoxical redeployment of this particular quote. In lifting out the quote to call for a moment of glory was Reagan forgetting the failure and the bloody deaths the speech portends? If so, how does such forgetting, or such (mis)remembering, or such theatrical redeployment of theatre, become historical fact or relevant to the historian? As I wrote in *Performing Remains*, we may recall here that John L. O'Sullivan, the coiner of the phrase "Manifest Destiny," could claim as late as 1839 that he and his fellow Americans had no memory of battlefields – in a country "won" by significant bloodshed of native Americans.

> It is our unparalleled glory that we have no reminiscences of battle fields [...] Who then can doubt that our country is destined to be the great nation of futurity? (1839: 427, 430)

In what became a very famous quote, O'Sullivan advocated forgetting, erasure, and ignorance as vital ingredients for the making of America's future. For take careful note: O'Sullivan did not claim that there were no battlefields, only that there would be no memory of them. If this is an insight philosopher Friedrich Nietzsche spelled out in 1873 in "On the Uses and Disadvantages of History for Life" (1997) – that any history is also a forgetting – in 1882 Ernst Renan, a philosopher and historian of early Christianity, observed:

> [...] forgetting, I would even go so far as to say historical error, is a crucial factor in the creation of a nation, which is why progress in historical studies often constitutes a danger for [the principle of] nationality. (1990: 11)

O'Sullivan, Nietzsche, Renan, and Reagan all help us recall that the future is often carved out by manipulating faults and crafting errors in recall. If time "marches on" toward claims we place on its direction, it clearly does not march in step with fact, nor hardly in a straight line, but across minefields of purposeful forgetting, misrecognition, blatant erasure, and false posturing. To explore a nation's history, its construction and transmission as nation, is necessarily to engage in an analysis of the generative properties of false recall – of the (mis)telling in retelling – the "real" as forged by the "faux" – and this, it seems to me, suggests that the history of any nation is a theatre history.

If the historian's aim is to untangle the forgetting from the remembering, or distinguish the fake from the real to get at a true story, and the theatre's (or politician's, or nation's) aim is to confuse the borders again to truly tell a story, the best way to do *either* might be to acknowledge the ways in which the theatrical and the historical are, at all moments, profoundly and fundamentally co-constitutive. And as always, minor historical facts themselves can lead to ever more thorny problems concerning the borders between fake and real. Consider this interesting factoid: late in his life O'Sullivan became a practicing Spiritualist. Spiritualism was a religious practice with millions of followers at its peak in the US between the 1840s and the 1920s, based on the belief that the spirits of the dead communicate with the living through mediums. Many prominent Spiritualists, such as the Fox sisters, were women who supported abolitionism and women's suffrage. Their spirit guides were often "dead Indians" (McGarry 2008: 66–93). In the late 1870s, O'Sullivan claimed to have used the services of one Martha Fox to communicate with William Shakespeare from beyond the grave (Sampson 2003: 234). If so, what did Shakespeare say? O'Sullivan doesn't tell us. *This*, of course, adds even more tangled complications to our delicate (im)balance between theatre and history, real and faux, bodily passion and adequate mental idea. Again: might "real" access to the dead, and thus historical information, be open via portals of possession trance, for instance? If the answer is an absolute "no," how so? Who is to legislate the "fact" or "fiction" of such performance-based experiences? Who is to navigate the incredibly tangled geopolitics that finds Native American guides purportedly speaking through possessed Caucasian suffragettes working against the slavery of African Americans?

Shakespeare? One wonders that O'Sullivan wasn't visited in a Spiritualist session by the Chickasaw, Choctaw, Creek, Seminole, and Cherokee who died in the 1830s on the Trail of Tears or in the many skirmishes and battles O'Sullivan presciently claimed that "America" would not remember. But then, perhaps he *was* so visited – but chose not to recall it in his letters. As James Wilkinson reminds us: "not everything in the past has left traces" (1996: 80). Might such a "forgotten" conversation nevertheless be recounted by an historian? If not by an historian, then by whom? A playwright, perhaps.

In *Death by Drama And Other Medieval Legends*, theatre and literary historian Jody Enders has been eloquent on the matter of the tangle between the faux and the real, especially as concerns life and death.

> With all due respect to James Wilkinson's intelligent reminder that "not everything in the past has left traces," there were traces of medieval and Renaissance drama all over the place. It was a question of how to decipher them – or, as Jean-Claude Schmidt declared of the difficulty of approaching medieval culture – "not so much a question of sources as of cognitive tools for decoding them." [...] Any history of the Western stage and any historiography of the Middle Ages would have to take into account the absolutely precocious ways in which early France told, retold, invented and reinvented stories of the

tenuous boundaries between theatre and real life. (2002: xxiv)

Enders cites de Certeau, who wrote that historiography "oscillates between producing history and telling stories without being reducible to either one or the other" (2002: xxv). As an historian she charts her own wrestling with this oscillation and attempts, as a strategy, to keep the oscillation in play, in fact to explore the oscillation as itself historical fact – oscillation being "what happened." In *The Medieval Theater of Cruelty*, Enders thinks deeply about one story of a theatre event that took place in the city of Tournai in France in 1549. The story comes to us that during a playing of the biblical drama of Judith and Holofernes,

> [...] the "actor" playing Judith actually beheaded a convicted murderer who had briefly assumed the "role" of Holofernes (the doomed Assyrian general in the story) – long enough to be killed during the "play" to thunderous applause. (1999: 203)

For this to have happened, the knife used and the blood spilt in the death of Holofernes had to have been "real." And still, contra Abramović, it would also have been theatre – though Enders places words like "actor," "role," and "play" in quotation marks because players and characters were often fabulously intertwined in medieval practice, making the clear dividing lines that we assume today seem far murkier to assess. But the conclusions Enders draws are very interesting and deserve quoting at length. (Note that she, too, turns to Rome.) First – *if* the Tournai story is true:

> If true, Tournai provides proof of Kenneth Burke's suggestions that "the symbolic act of art overlaps upon the symbolic act of life" and of [Anthony] Kubiak's suggestion that "we forget that theatre is the primary condition of life, that life itself is 'always already' subsumed by the theatrical." If true, this moment would be part of the larger history of torture, which included the "castigation with rods, scourging, and bow with chains" enumerated in the Justinian *Digest*. For if the Tournai criminal really died, he resembled all too closely the "actors" in Roman gladiatorial display who "affect dying even as death really occurs ... [and] become actors who die for the pleasure of their spectators, and what seems worse, who must perform their own deaths with broad theatrical strokes." And he would render it possible to speak of real coercion, real performativity, real "speech acts" on the medieval stage. If there was at least the possibility that real death might occur on stage, then any line within a play calling for brutality, torture, punishment or death would not merely *describe* doing something. In the strict Austinian sense, it would actually *do* something: "the issuing of the utterance is

the performing of an action – it is not normally thought of as just saying something." (1999: 205, emphasis in original)

If there is even the possibility of truth to the story, she concludes, then there is the possibility of this tenuous border between theatre and real life extending to blood and knives and practices of torture on the stage and beyond the stage. The "might have happened" becomes as powerful as the "did happen." We can see this even more clearly in her provocative suggestion of what it would mean *if* the Tournai story is false:

> If false, Tournai testifies to the existence of a kind of medieval urban legend just as frightening [...] As such, it would have functioned as a myth which, then and now, disclosed more about the spectators' fears about what *could* happen in the theater than about what actually did happen. [...] [W]hether or not the death at Tournai actually happened, the mere investigation of that question irrevocably compromises certain generic cornerstones of theater [...]: the illusion of theater's civility, the viability of catharsis, and the entire principle of moral or aesthetic distance which collapses under the weight of performativity. In a world where legends about on-stage executions circulated, where public executions were orchestrated and attended as spectacles,

and where the language of theater replicated the confusion between impersonation and reality, one troublesome conclusion would be that as a genre, early drama was tied to the larger history of torture, justice, punishment, and even the regulation of public entertainments. The possibility of real violence in Tournai would then resonate with such events as the following: certain French medieval Bishops were empowered to force men to accept Christ through flogging – the same ecclesiastical dignitaries who might have been watching theatrical spectacles from on high. (1999: 205–8, emphasis in original)

Enders acknowledges that there is obviously something deeply and profoundly different and at stake for the historical record (let alone for the "actor" and "audience" involved!) if an actual death took place. And, as historians, doing our best to account for when and where the blood was fake or the blood was real is essential to our endeavor. Nevertheless, when stories and urban legends carry the death as real, whether or not it was literally real does not fully, not entirely alter the historical agency, the power, of the story transmitted. Sometimes what is powerful historically is that real death *might have happened*, and whether or not it did Enders makes clear that the "might have happened" and "might yet happen" are part of the truth-effects that storytelling and theatre have on their historical audiences. Then as now, the "real" often becomes itself in the wake of the "false," and vice versa. Thus Enders calls for an interdisciplinary approach to the question of mimesis that acknowledges the "inherently mimetic propensities of human beings" (2005: xxvii) and looks to the residue of theatricality in all human traces, as well as the residue of historicity transmitted through theatrical tradition.

* * *

At the close of this inquiry, what can we say? Even if we cannot fully trust the fake knife not to draw real blood, or fake blood not to displace real violence, is it safe to say that in the passageways between theatre's nows and history's thens there is expansive room for conversation? If, some-times, speaking across disciplinary and medial boundaries is confusing – different disciplines and different media have different languages, different investments, different out-comes – we shouldn't forget that it's often in the babble of different languages that "new" ideas, "new" theories, "new" practices are hatched and "old" ideas, "old" theories, "old" practices might be rediscovered.

Performance studies scholar Shannon Jackson relates one fact of the matter: communication across disciplines, especially academic disciplines in relation to theatre, can produce encounters that are often "awkward." Folks don't always speak the same language – far from it. As we've seen, in the disciplinary tensions between thinking and feeling and doing that inflect history and theatre differently, there lurks all manner of antitheatricality and related anti-intellectualism that can make discussions between theorists and practitioners, historians and actors, scholars and artists strained at best. At times, sitting on one's hands or just walling up inside the black box feels preferable to trying to communicate. What can we possibly have to say to each other when "Don't' think– feel!" is one motto and "Don't feel – think!" is another? Both are *passionate* investments, but they appear to want to cancel each other out. Add to this that, as we have seen, when we really dig into the matter of the ampersand between our terms, it seems like paradoxes simply reduplicate without resolution. So, of course cross-disciplinary exploration will be awkward – at best! But, Jackson writes, "I happen to believe that it is necessary to both analyze the dispositions that produce that awkwardness as well as to embrace awkwardness as a condition of emergence" (2004: 2).

So, why study theatre history? Why sit awkwardly on your hands if you are an actor? Why get awkwardly to your feet as an historian? To embrace awkwardness as a means to emergence? Maybe. You will make up your own reasons on your journey in the sets of tracks (know them or not) that you inherit. It is not, after all, any more radically strange or awkward to suggest that theatre and performance artists are historians than it is to suggest that historians are purveyors of theatricality, if theatricality means, at least in part, the employment of a surrogate to stand in for something it is not. Words – the stuff of many histories – are like actors. They pose as if the thing itself, and strut and fret their stories across the stages of books, essays, and documentaries, bringing the past, again, to life. Or – a kind of life. A *theatrical* life composed in the ambivalences of temporalities.

Theatre and performance may, after all, compose the itinerant life of the real – where something that may have happened in one time reappears, sometimes radically disguised, in another time. Theatre is a survival *of sorts*. Sorting the survivals, parsing the faux from the real, and re-placing the real in the faux must take account of displacement and replacement as the mode of any and all communication. The temporal travels of things, signs, and signs of signs can wash history up on the unlikely shores of our theatre stages just as often as strand it behind glass in our object-based archives. Certainly, considering seriously the reliability or unreliability of bodily forms – *theatrical* flotsam and jetsam – will require rigorous analysis of the ampersand between fake and real, remembering and forgetting, live and dead.

The couple Historicity and Theatricality cannot divide their children among them, for new children are born everyday wherever sameness takes place again as difference, difference as sameness. This is what playwright Amiri Baraka in *Black Music* called the "changing same" (1968: 232). Better to consider the triplets of Thinking, Feeling, and Doing together – umbilically, paradoxically, and indeterminably syncopated – if we are to make meaningful sense(ations) of ourselves both forward and backward (and as theatrical aside) in time.

notes

1. Among many books on theatre historiography see Canning and Postlewait 2010; Bial and Magelssen 2010; Postlewait 2009. Other key texts will be cited throughout.
2. As James Wilkinson reminds us, "Few historians today would claim that it is possible to create a history that exactly mimics the past, a history *wie es eigentlich gewesen [ist]* 'as it actually happened,' in the optimistic and much cited phrase of the nineteenth-century German Historian Leopold von Ranke" (1996: 80).
3. And, *conj. Oxford English Dictionary*. Aug. 2013 <http://www.oed.com>. All dictionary definitions that follow will be taken from the *OED*.
4. A note on the word "orature." The word was coined by Ugandan scholar Pio Zirimu. For a sense of the deeper conversation the word invites, see Ngũgĩ wa Thiong'o 2007. Important work on thinking through (or beyond or without) the sometimes false legislation of borders between orality and textuality has been amply generated in the journal *Callaloo*, with key attention to the African diaspora.
5. See <http://www.lincolnpresenters.net/abelist.html>.
6. Some texts that explore and debate relations between history and reenactment are Phillips, Caine, and Thomas 2013; Dray 1999; McCalman and Pickering 2010; Magelssen and Justice-Malloy 2011; Schneider 2011.

7. Throughout this book I avoid a definitive parsing of the terms "memory" and "history," though it is arguably vital to the conversation. The distinction has often devolved to history as textual and associated with institutional archives versus memory (the poor relation) as linked to a fleshly body or collective of bodies. Not tied to "fact," memory is prone to error and composed in performance's repetitions. If "history" and "theatre" seem both related and opposed to each other, as we are exploring in this book, those relations and oppositions are often synonymous with the ways in which history and memory can be called "colliding worlds" (Wineburg 2000: 321). On the stakes involved in distinctions between history and memory see Foucault 1977; Roach 1996; Ricoeur 2006: 396–97; Nyong'o 2009; Schneider 2011: 36–39. On memory and mistake see Nyong'o 2009: 135–66. On "collective memory" see Halbwachs 1992 and the helpful exegesis in Connerton 1989.

8. The practice of history in the West emerges as what Georg G. Iggers describes as the "conscious effort" to "distinguish history from myth and to arrive at a truthful description of past events." Other birthing sites, separating history from prehistory, occurred around the globe and shared in the "conscious effort" that resulted in records. This "effort" occurred "at least as early as Herodotus and Thucydides in the West and Ssu'ma Chi'en in the East" (1997: 17).

9. As early as 1926, the historian Carl Becker, sometimes called a "pre-postmodernist," wrote an influential essay titled "What Are Historical Facts?" Perhaps in response to the First World War, he concluded that there are none (see Wright 2000). For Becker, this was not to say that there is no history or that nothing can be accounted for, but to provoke us to analyze our inevitable entanglements in the processes of interpretation and communication that complicate facticity.

10. Indian theatre traditions orient the audience to "rasa" – taste or flavor – as a sense at the base of theatre (Miller 1984: 14). Yoruban ritual traditions have been said to emphasize rhythm (Drewal 1992: 2–3). Greek philosophy and dramatic texts clearly privilege "sight" as a metaphor for knowledge, but sound was essential in the actual practice of ancient theatre, as were music and dance. Also consider that many Asian, African, and indigenous American theatrical

lineages do not segregate dance, musical, and spoken drama as distinct traditions.

11. According to Fischer-Lichte: "Theatricality may be defined as a particular mode of using signs or as a particular kind of semiotic process in which particular signs (human beings and objects of their environment) are employed as signs of signs – by their producers, or their recipients. Thus a shift of the dominance within the semiotic functions determines when theatricality appears. When the semiotic function of using signs as signs of signs in a behavioural, situational or communication process is perceived and received as dominant, the behavioural, situational or communication process may be regarded as theatrical. Moreover, since this shift of the dominant is not an objective given but depends on certain pragmatic conditions, 'theatricality' in the end, appears to be no more than a floating signifier in an endless communication process. This is to say that the term theatricality necessarily remains diffuse; as a concept it becomes indistinct, if not void" (1995: 88). See also Feral 2002.

12. Throughout, and in the interest of brevity, I use the words "affect," "feelings," "emotion," and "passion" somewhat interchangeably. But there are many debates, most of them unresolved, on distinctions between the terms. A great deal is at stake in "affect" in contemporary theories about virtual reality and historical study. Some scholars, such as Brian Massumi (2002), want to separate affect from emotion, reserving affect for realms of autonomous sensation and emotion for feelings linked with personal histories. Sara Ahmed (2004) rejects this perspective and sees the terms an indelibly interrelated. See also Gorton 2007; Gregg and Seigworth 2010; Hurley 2010.

13. In his introduction to *Method Acting Reconsidered*, an anthology responding to criticisms of method acting, David Krasner reminds his readers that altering Stanislavsky should not be considered a crime – think of Meyerhold, Vakhtangov, and Grotowski (2000: 29).

14. Elizabeth Hapgood translated the Russian *perezhivanie*, which means "experiencing," from the root *zhit* ("to live"), as "living a part" (Carnicke 1998: 109). The concept of *perezhivanie*, at the heart of Stanislavsky's system, allowed actors to gauge "the genuine

penetration of a psychic state in a represented character" (1998: 109). In an excellent review of five turn-of-the-twenty-first-century books on Stanislavsky's "system" and the American "method," Tracy C. Davis tells us that in the United States "because of mistranslation, this crucial idea [of *perezhivanie*] disappeared in lieu of schismatic debates about emotional/affective memory, objectives, and motivations. Whereas Stanislavsky recognized acting's irony of being 'true' through creation of another – like Diderot, finding a divided consciousness of actor and role – Lee Strasberg [architect, with Meisner and others, of Stanislavsky-derived method acting] rejected all but genuine experience and absolute sincerity" (2001: 373). Note that here it is the field of debate Davis is interested in, rather than definitive interpretation of a master. Davis's review helpfully situates the ongoing stakes concerning what constitutes "good acting," especially as concerns the "authenticity of what an actor *feels* while acting" (2001: 371), as those debates continue even today to crystallize around the paradigm of "Stanislavsky."

15. I adopt, here, Kenneth Burke's (1969) expanded definition of rhetoric.

16. Barish 1985. See the special issue of *Modern Drama* devoted to a critical appraisal of Barish's work (Ackerman 2001).

17. Another of Stanislavsky's students, Vsevolod Meyerhold (1978), argued for artificiality and stylization as theatre's true art, reminding us that Stanislavsky's lineage is not limited to his own "disgust" with the artificial. In fact, on his deathbed, Stanislavsky named Meyerhold his best student, indeed "my sole heir in the theatre – here or anywhere else" (cited in Rudnitsky 1981: xv).

18. Mary Keller has written on the gendered aspects of possession: "Religious traditions in which people are possessed have existed throughout recorded history and continue to exist on all continents of the globe. Women predominate in these accounts, and their predominance is noted by many scholars who attribute it to women's inferior gendered status in patriarchal culture. [...] The power of her possessed body is reduced to 'hysteria' at worst and creative therapy at best. The key to the problem is not that possession studies are sexist or racist but that a social scientific method is unable to take seriously what the witnesses to the possession say is the case – that

the power that overcomes them comes from an ancestor, deity, or spirit" (2002: 2–3). Though recent scholars have begun to take possession seriously as "real," she notes, they do so by describing possession as "forms of theater," mitigating the claim to the real (2002: 46).

19.   Interestingly, "worlding" does not appear in the *Oxford English Dictionary*, but in the glossary to Paul Knox and Steven Pinch's *Urban Social Geography: An Introduction* we find "worlding" defined as "The discourse used to represent colonized territories. May be used to describe the ways in which any place is represented" (2009: xx).

20.   Hegel 1956: 99. Hegel did not claim that peoples without history are people without writing, but people who lack statehood. See Ranajit Guha's analysis of the ways in which historiography subordinated and subsumed subaltern people into narratives of Empire and Nation that relegate the subaltern to "peoples without history" (2002: xx).

21.   Cultural historians now accept popular and aesthetic representation generally as social modes of historicization, often under Maurice Halbwachs's (1992) rubric "collective memory." Still, the process of approaching aesthetic production as valid historiography involves careful (and debated) delineation between "memory," "myth," "ritual," and "tradition" on the one hand and the implicitly more legitimate (or supposedly non-mythic) "history" on the other. See Kammen 1993: 25–32.

22.   The twenty-first century has seen many books wrestling with this question from within theatre and performance studies, troubling the boundaries of the disciplines of theatre and history, as well as the boundaries between recording or document and theatre. For a cursory list, in addition to Taylor 2003, see Forsyth and Megson 2009; Pearson and Shanks 2001; Rokem 2002; Martin 2012.

23.   Resources on modes of access for materials "hidden from history" are vast. Some scholars look to live performance and affective engagement as places for excavation. Odai Johnson (2009) reads play scripts of Roman comedy for what they do not say, looking for the "double-voice" of slaves (on double-voice see Gates 1989). This survival of the unsaid is often recuperable in performance, and Johnson looks through or beyond the playtext to the bodies engaged.

On using affective engagement as a mode of queer historiography where "records" may disguise, hide, or deny libidinal embodied life see Dinshaw 1999.

24. Halliwell prefers the translation "representation" rather than "imitation." It might be argued that not all theatre is mimetic. Not all theatre "represents." Consider Peter Brook's claim that "I can take any empty space and call it a bare stage. A man walks across this empty space whilst someone else is watching him, and this is all that is needed for an act of theatre to be engaged" (2008: 11). For Brook the "act" of theatre is the naming of a stage and the presence of an audience, making spectatorship *of anything* theatre, without hypothesis beyond the claim "this is a stage" and the presence of watcher and watched. In other words, if nothing is imitated or represented on stage, it is still theatre. The minute we ask, however, whether the act of walking or the act of viewing "tells us something" – anything – we have triggered mimesis in the equation. And the minute we try to relate *What Happened* on Brook's stage (to borrow the title from Gertrude Stein's first play), we have engaged mimesis, if not imitation.

25. On non-imitative mimesis in Indian theatre see Miller 1894: 19.

26. For accounts of the shared history see Puchner 2010; Stern 2013: 75–77.

27. Hand stencils made by blowing paint onto cave walls, sometimes called "negative hands," date as far back as 40,800 years.

28. The appellation "live art" is commonly associated with performance art, or time-based arts, and it came into use in the UK in the 1980s to define a wide umbrella of "experimental" artworks involving living performers or artists in time-based works. Because much "live art" as defined since the 1980s does not necessarily rely on play scripts, as the trajectory of a great deal (but not all) of Western theatrical art had done for thousands of years, some would prefer the terms "live art" and "performance art" to remain in distinction to "theatre."

29. Alan Ackerman has written that Reagan's political "triumph" signified "less a new privileging of the actor than a rhetorical shift whereby the very idiom of theatricality has shifted from the marginal to the normative" (2001: 277).

bibliography

Ackerman, Alan. 2001. "Introduction: Modernism and Antitheatricality." *Modern Drama* 44.3: 275–83.

Ahmed, Sara. 2004. *The Cultural Politics of Emotion*. Edinburgh: Edinburgh UP.

Aristotle. 1987. *The Poetics of Aristotle*. Trans. Stephen Halliwell. Chapel Hill: U of North Carolina P.

Artaud, Antonin. 1994. *The Theatre and Its Double*. Trans. Mary Caroline Richards. New York: Grove.

Austin, J. L. 1975. *How to Do Things with Words*. 2nd ed. Cambridge, MA: Harvard UP.

Baraka, Amiri (LeRoi Jones). 1968. *Black Music*. New York: William Morrow.

Barish, Jonas. 1985. *The Antitheatrical Prejudice*. Berkeley: U of California P.

Barthes, Roland. 1981. "The Discourse of History." *Comparative Criticism: A Yearbook* 3: 3–28.

Berlant, Lauren. 2008. *The Female Complaint: The Unfinished Business of Sentimentality in American Culture*. Durham, NC: Duke UP.

Bial, Henry, and Scott Magelssen, eds. 2010. *Theater Historiography: Critical Interventions*. Ann Arbor: U of Michigan P.

Brook, Peter. 2008. *The Empty Space*. New York: Penguin.

Burke, Kenneth. 1969. *A Grammar of Motives*. Berkeley: U of California P.

Canning, Charlotte, and Thomas Postlewait, eds. 2010. *Representing the Past: Essays in Performance Historiography*. Iowa City: U of Iowa P.

Carlson, Marvin. 2001. *The Haunted Stage: The Theatre as Memory Machine*. Ann Arbor: U of Michigan P.

Carnicke, Sharon. 2000. "Stanislavsky's System: Pathways for the Actor." *Twentieth Century Actor Training*. Ed. A. Hodge. London: Routledge. 11–36.

———. 1998. *Stanislavsky in Focus*. Amsterdam: Harwood.

de Certeau, Michel. 1986. "History: Science and Fiction." *Heterologies: Discourse on the Other*. Trans. Brian Massumi. Minneapolis: U of Minnesota P. 199–224.

Collingwood, R. G. 1994. *The Idea of History*. Ed. Jan van der Dussen. New York: Oxford UP.

Connerton, Paul. 1989. *How Societies Remember*. Cambridge: Cambridge UP.

Critchlow, Donald T., and Nancy MacLean. 2009. *Debating the American Conservative Movement, 1945 to the Present*. Lanham, MD: Rowman & Littlefield.

Davis, Tracy C. 2001. "*Stanislavsky in Focus* by Sharon M. Carnicke, and: *Twentieth Century Actor Training* ed. by Alison Hodge, and: *Acting Emotions: Shaping Emotions on Stage* by Elly A. Konijn, and: *Method Acting Reconsidered: Theory, Practice, Future* ed. by David Krasner, and: *On Actors and Acting* by Peter Thomson (review)." *Modern Drama* 44.3: 369–79.

Derrida, Jacques. 1998. *Archive Fever: A Freudian Impression*. Chicago, IL: U of Chicago P.

Diderot, Denis. 1994. "The Paradox of the Actor." 1773. *Selected Writings on Art and Literature*. Trans. Geoffrey Bremer. London: Penguin. 98–158.

Dinshaw, Carolyn. 1999. *Getting Medieval: Sexualilties and Communities Pre- and Postmodern*. Durham, NC: Duke UP.

Dray, William H. 1999. *History as Reenactment: R. G. Collingwood's Idea of History*. Oxford: Clarendon.

Drewal, Margaret Thompson. 1992. *Yoruba Ritual: Performers, Play, Agency*. Bloomington: Indiana UP.

Enders, Jody. 2005. *Death by Drama And Other Medieval Legends*. Chicago, IL: U of Chicago P.

————. 1999. *The Medieval Theater of Cruelty*. Ithaca, NY: Cornell UP.

Evans, J. A. S. 1968. "Father of History or Father of Lies; The Reputation of Herodotus." *The Classical Journal* 64.1: 11–17.

Feral, Josette. 2002. Foreword. *Theatricality*. Spec. issue of *SubStance* 31: 2–3.

Fischer-Lichte, Erika. 2002. *History of European Drama and Theatre*. Trans. Jo Riley. New York: Routledge.

————. 1995. "Introduction: Theatricality: A Key Concept in Theatre and Cultural Studies." *Theatre Research International* 20.2: 85–89.

————. 2008. "Shared Bodies, Shared Spaces: The Bodily Co-Presence of Actors and Spectators." *The Transformative Power of Performance*. New York: Routledge. 38–74.

Forsyth, Alison, and Chris Megson, eds. 2009. *Documentary Theatre Past and Present*. New York: Palgrave Macmillan.

Foucault, Michel. 1972. *The Archaeology of Knowledge*. Trans. Alan Sheridan. London: Tavistock.

————. 1977. "Nietzsche, Genealogy, History." *Language, Countermemory, Practice*. Trans. Donald F. Bouchard. Ithaca, NY: Cornell UP. 139–64.

Freud, Sigmund. 1990. *Beyond the Pleasure Principle*. Trans. James Strachey. New York: Norton.

Garber, Marjorie. 2008. *Profiling Shakespeare*. New York: Routledge.

Gates, Henry Lewis. 1989. *The Signifying Monkey: A Theory of African American Literary Criticism*. New York: Oxford UP.

Geertz, Clifford. 1977. *The Interpretation of Cultures*. New York: Basic.

Gorton, Kristyn. 2007. "Theorizing Emotion and Affect: Feminist Engagements." *Feminist Theory* 8.3: 333–48.

Greenblatt, Stephen. 1980. *Renaissance Self-Fashioning: From More to Shakespeare*. Chicago, IL: U of Chicago P.

————. 1989. *Shakespearean Negotiations*. Berkeley: U of California P.

Gregg, Melissa, and Gregory J. Seigworth. 2010. *The Affect Theory Reader*. Durham, NC: Duke UP.

Guha, Ranajit. 2002. *History at the Limit of World History*. New York: Columbia UP.

Gupt, Bharat. 1994. *Dramatic Concepts Greek and Indian: A Study of Poetics and Natyasastra*. New Delhi: D.K. Printworld.

Halbwachs, Maurice. 1992. *On Collective Memory*. Trans. Lewis A. Coser. Chicago, IL: U of Chicago P.

Halliwell, Stephen. 2002. *The Aesthetics of Mimesis: Ancient Texts and Modern Problems*. Princeton, NJ: Princeton UP.

Harries, Martin. 2000. *Scare Quotes from Shakespeare: Marx, Keynes, and the Language of Reenchantment*. Palo Alto, CA: Stanford UP.

Hartog, François. 1988. *The Mirror of Herodotus*. Trans. Janet Lloyd. Berkeley: U of California P.

Hegel, Georg Wilhelm Friedrich. 1956. *The Philosophy of History*. New York: Dover.

Hurley, Erin. 2010. *Theatre & Feeling*. Basingstoke, UK: Palgrave Macmillan.

Iggers, Georg G. 1997. *Historiography in the Twentieth Century: From Scientific Objectivity to the Postmodern Challenge*. Hanover, NH: Wesleyan UP.

Jackson, Shannon. 2004. *Professing Performance: Theater in the Academy from Philology to Performativity*. Cambridge: Cambridge UP.

Johnson, Odai. 2009. "Unspeakable Histories: Terror, Spectacle, and Genocidal Memory." *Modern Language Quarterly* 70.1: 97–116.

Jones, Andrew Merion. 2012. "Living Rocks: Animacy, Performance and the Rock Art of the Kilmartin Region." *Visualizing the Neolithic*. Ed. Andrew Cochrane and Andrew Merion Jones. Oxford: Oxbow. 79–88.

Kammen, Michael. 1993. *Mystic Chords of Memory: The Transformation of Tradition in American Culture*. New York: Vintage.

Keller, Mary. 2002. *The Hammer and the Flute: Women, Power, and Spirit Possession*. Baltimore, MD: Johns Hopkins UP.

Knox, Paul, and Steven Pinch. 2009. *Urban Social Geography: An Introduction*. New York: Routledge.

Krasner, David, ed. 2000. *Method Acting Reconsidered: Theory, Practice, Future*. New York: St. Martin's.

LaCapra, Dominick. 1985. "Rhetoric and History." *History and Criticism*. Ithaca, NY: Cornell UP. 15–44.

———. 2001. *Writing History, Writing Trauma*. Baltimore, MD: Johns Hopkins UP.

Lamb, Jonathan. 2008. "Historical Reenactment, Extremity, and Passion." *The Eighteenth Century* 49.3: 239–50.

————. 2010. "Introduction to Settlers, Creoles, and Historical Reenactment." *Settlers, Creoles, and Historical Reenactment*. Ed. Vanessa Agnew and Jonathan Lamb. New York: Palgrave Macmillan. 1–18.

Laurel, Brenda. 2013. *Computers as Theatre*. 2nd ed. Indianapolis, IN: Addison-Wesley.

Le Goff, Jacques. 1992. *History and Memory*. Trans. Steven Rendall and Elizabeth Claman. New York: Columbia UP.

Leprohon, Ronald J. 2007. "Ritual Drama in Ancient Egypt." *The Origins of Theatre in Ancient Greece and Beyond*. Ed. Erik Csapo and Margaret C. Miller. Cambridge: Cambridge UP. 259–92.

Levine, Laura. 1994. *Men in Women's Clothing: Anti-Theatricality and Effeminization 1579–1642*. Cambridge: Cambridge UP.

Longwell, Dennis, and Sanford Meisner. 1987. *Sanford Meisner on Acting*. New York: Vintage.

Magelssen, Scott, and Rhona Justice-Malloy, eds. 2011. *Enacting History*. Birmingham: U of Alabama P.

Martin, Carol, ed. 2012. *Dramaturgy of the Real on the World Stage*. New York: Palgrave Macmillan.

Massumi, Brian. 2002. *Parables of the Virtual: Movement, Affect, Sensation*. Durham, NC: Duke UP.

McCalman, Ian, and Paul A. Pickering. 2010. *Historical Reenactment: From Realism to the Affective Turn*. New York: Palgrave Macmillan.

McGarry, Molly. 2008. "Indian Guides: Haunted Subjects and the Politics of Vanishing." *Ghosts of Futures Past: Spiritualism and the Cultural Politics of Nineteenth-Century America*. Berkeley: U of California P. 66–93.

Meyerhold, Vsevolod. 1978. *Meyerhold on Theatre*. Trans. Edward Braun. New York: Bloomsbury Methuen Drama.

Michals, Teresa. 2010. "'Like a Spoiled Actress off the Stage': Antitheatricality, Nature, and the Novel." *Studies in Eighteenth Century Culture* 39: 191–214.

Miller, Barbara Stoler. 1984. *Theatres of Memory: Kalidasa's World and His Plays*. New York: Columbia UP.

Montelle, Yann-Pierre. 2009. *Palaeoperformance: The Emergence of Theatricality as Social Practice*. Calcutta: Seagull.

Morris, Brian. 2006. *Religion and Anthropology: A Critical Introduction*. Cambridge: Cambridge UP.

Nietzsche, Friedrich. 1997. "On the Uses and Disadvantages of History for Life." 1873. *Untimely Meditations*. Ed. Daniel Breazeale. Trans. R. Hollingdale. Cambridge: Cambridge UP. 57–124.

Nyong'o, Tavia. 2009. *Amalgamation Waltz: Race, Performance, and the Ruses of Memory*. Minneapolis: U of Minnesota P.

O'Hagan, Sean. 2010. "Interview: Marina Abramović." *The Guardian* 2 Oct. <http://www.theguardian.com/artanddesign/2010/oct/03/interview-marina-abramovic-performance-artist#history-link-box>.

O'Sullivan, John L. 1839. "The Great Nation of Futurity." *United States Magazine and Democratic Review* 6.23 (Nov.): 426–30.

Pearson, Mike, and Theodore Shanks. 2001. *Theatre/Archaeology*. New York: Routledge.

Phillips, Mark Salber, Barbara Caine, and Julia Adeney Thomas, eds. 2013. *Rethinking Historical Distance*. New York: Palgrave Macmillan.

Postlewait, Thomas. 2009. *The Cambridge Introduction to Theatre Historiography*. Cambridge: Cambridge UP.

Puchner, Martin. 2010. *The Drama of Ideas: Platonic Provocations in Theater and Philosophy*. Oxford: Oxford UP.

Renan, Ernst. 1990. "What Is a Nation?" [1882]. *Nation and Narration*. Ed. Homi Bhabha. New York: Routledge. 8–22.

Richmond, Farley P. 1990. "The Origins of Sanskrit Drama." *Indian Theatre: Traditions of Performance*. Ed. Farley P. Richmond, Darius L. Swan, and Phillip B. Zarrilli. Honolulu: U of Hawaii P. 25–32.

Ricoeur, Paul. 2006. *History, Memory, Forgetting*. Trans. Kathleen Blamey and David Pellauer. Chicago, IL: U of Chicago P.

Ridout, Nicholas. 2006. *Stage Fright, Animals, and Other Theatrical Problems*. New York: Cambridge UP.

Ritchie, Donald. 2003. *Doing Oral History*. 2nd ed. New York: Oxford UP.

Roach, Joseph. 1996. *Cities of the Dead: Circum-Atlantic Performance*. New York: Columbia UP.

———. 1993. *The Player's Passion: Studies in the Science of Acting*. Ann Arbor: U of Michigan P.

Rokem, Freddie. 2002. *Performing History: Theatrical Representations of the Past in Contemporary Theatre*. Ames: U of Iowa P.

Rowbotham, Sheila. 1973. *Hidden from History: Rediscovering Women in History from the 17th Century to the Present*. New York: Vintage.

Rudnitsky, Konstantin. 1981. *Meyerhold the Director*. Trans. George Petrov. Ed. Sydney Schultze. Introd. Ellendea Proffer. Ann Arbor, MI: Ardis.

Sampson, Robert D. 2003. *John L. O'Sullivan and His Times*. Kent, OH: Kent State UP.

Schechner, Richard. 2013. *Introduction to Performance Studies*. New York: Routledge.

———. 1988. *Performance Theory*. New York: Routledge.

Schneider, Rebecca. 2011. *Performing Remains: Art and War in Times of Theatrical Reenactment*. New York: Routledge.

Silverman, Kaja. 1996. *Thresholds of the Visible World*. New York: Routledge.

Sofer, Andrew. 2003. *The Stage Life of Props*. Ann Arbor: U of Michigan P.

Stallybrass, Peter, and Ann Rosalind Jones. 2001. "Fetishizing the Glove in Renaissance Europe." *Critical Inquiry* 28.1: 114–32.

Stanislavski, Konstantin. 1989. *An Actor Prepares*. Trans. Elizabeth R. Hapgood. New York: Routledge.

States, Bert O. 1987. *Great Reckonings in Little Rooms: On the Phenomenology of Theater*. Berkeley: U of California P.

Stein, Gertrude. 1935. *Lectures in America*. New York: Random House.

Stern, Tom. 2013. *Philosophy and Theatre: An Introduction*. New York: Routledge.

Stoller, Ann Laura. 2009. *Along the Archival Grain: Epistemic Anxieties and Colonial Common Sense*. Princeton, NJ: Princeton UP.

Taylor, Diana. 2003. *The Archive and the Repertoire*. Durham, NC: Duke UP.

wa Thiong'o, Ngũgĩ. 2007. "Notes toward a Performance Theory of Orature." *Performance Research* 12.3: 4–7.

Thomas, Richard. 1993. *The Imperial Archive: Knowledge and the Fantasy of Empire*. New York: Verso.

White, Hayden. 1978. *Tropics of Discourse*. Baltimore, MD: Johns Hopkins UP.

Wilkinson, James. 1996. "A Choice of Fictions: Historians, Memory, and Evidence." *PMLA* 111.1: 80–92.

Wills, Garry. 2011. *Rome and Rhetoric*. New Haven, CT: Yale UP.

Wineburg, Sam. 2000. "Making Historical Sense." *Knowing, Teaching, and Learning History*. Ed. Peter N. Stearns, Peter Seixas, and Sam Wineburg. New York: NYUP. 306–26.

Wright, Johnson Kent. 2000. "The Pre-Postmodernism of Carl Becker." *Postmodernism and the Enlightenment*. Trans. Daniel Gordon. New York: Routledge. 161–78.

Zhao, Shanyang. 2004. "Toward a Taxonomy of Co-Presence." *Presence* 12.5: 445–55.

Zumthor, Paul. 1990. *Oral Poetry: An Introduction*. Trans. Kathy Murphy-Judy. Minneapolis: U of Minnesota P.

For my mother, Pat Schneider,
in memory of her beloved friend
Elizabeth Berryhill, 1920–2002,
founder and director of the Straw Hat Review
and the Festival Theatre of San Anselmo, California

index

CPSIA information can be obtained
at www.ICGtesting.com
Printed in the USA
LVHW021050230222
711815LV00009BA/478